BLIND JACK
OF KNARESBOROUGH

A crude derivative portrait of Blind Jack (1810) emphasising his full height (6ft 2in).

BLIND JACK
OF KNARESBOROUGH

ARNOLD KELLETT

Acknowledgements

Thanks are due, first of all, to the Right Hon. David Blunkett, MP, for his foreword and his interest in launching and promoting the book – to say nothing of his own example in showing the same kind of Yorkshire grit and determination as John Metcalf.

Then I would like to acknowledge the helpfulness of archivists and librarians, especially those of the British Library (London and Boston Spa), the York Minster Library, the Borthwick Institute, the York City Archives, York Reference Library, West Yorkshire Archives, Wakefield, the North Yorkshire County Record Office, Northallerton, the Stockport Heritage Library, the Chester Record Office, the RNIB Reference Library, the Brotherton Library (Leeds University), Halifax Reference Library, Huddersfield Library, Knaresborough Town Council.

In addition, the following have kindly loaned material or produced useful information: Geoff Bowen, Janice Chatten, Geoffrey Craggs, Dr Ian Dewhirst, Peter Doyle, John Goodchild, Geoff Lawson, Ruth McCabe, The Metcalf Society, Malcolm Neesam, Mrs Gay Oliver (who has written a study of her ancestry, tracing it to John Metcalf, 'Spout House', 2002), Dr George Redmonds, Janet Riley, Ted Seed, John Symington, Dr Maurice Turner, Leonard Webster, and for warm encouragement from Dr Marc Maurer, president of the National Federation of the Blind, USA. For invaluable help with proof-reading, I am grateful to Peter Nelson and my daughter, Rachel Kidd.

Illustrations are mainly from my own collection of prints and photographs, but I am especially grateful to the Knaresborough-born painter, Barrington Bramley, who, at my request, generously reconstructed the contemporary portrait of Blind Jack as a superb oil-painting – to be presented to Knaresborough Town Council. I am also grateful to my friend Peter Kearney for so readily providing additional artwork.

As with all my books, the greatest indebtedness is to my wife, Pat, for her patience and unfailing support.

Arnold Kellett

First published 2008

Reprinted 2009

The History Press Ltd
The Mill, Brimscombe Port
Stroud, Gloucestershire, GL5 2QG
www.thehistorypress.co.uk

British Library Cataloguing in Publication Data.
A catalogue record for this book is available from the British Library.

ISBN 978 0 7524 4658 5

Typesetting and origination by
The History Press Ltd.
Printed and bound by TJ International Ltd, Padstow, Cornwall

Contents

Foreword by The Right Hon. David Blunkett, MP   6

Author's Preface   7

1. Birthplace and Early Childhood   8

2. From Teenage Escapades to Spa Musician   14

3. Taking the Waters: Huntsman, Guide, Bon Vivant   20

4. Amours and Adventures   28

5. Travels and Troubles: Love Finds a Way   36

6. Married Life: The Settled Years   44

7. The 1745 Rebellion: Military Musician   50

8. Into Battle: Prisoner of the Rebels   56

9. The Battle of Culloden, 16 April 1746   62

10. Trader, Smuggler, Wagoner: The First Road   70

11. Pioneer Road Builder   78

12. The Open Road: Profit and Loss   88

13. Towards the End of the Road   96

14. Opinion and Evaluation   108

Notes   118

Appendix A: Blind Jack's Music   127

Appendix B: Blind Jack's Roads   128

Foreword by the Right Hon. David Blunkett, MP

We owe Dr Arnold Kellett a debt of gratitude for pulling together the phenomenal story of John Metcalf, better known as Blind Jack.

For those who find his story so astonishing that they have difficulty in believing it, it is worth recalling that in this particular period of our history, the very early eighteenth century, there was, in fact, another phenomenal example of fortitude and almost unbelievable achievement. This was Nicholas Saunderson, who like Jack was blinded in early age through smallpox – and who rose to be president of the British Association, Professor of Mathematics at Cambridge, and a legend in his own time. He also was born in Yorkshire, just outside Penistone, to the north-west of Sheffield.

John Metcalf, musician, drinker, gambler, huntsman, horse-dealer, military adventurer, trader, smuggler and road builder, is testament to the unquelled human spirit. We have his own account of how the spur – the necessity of survival – led him into becoming larger than life, illustrating that we are what we are because of the experiences we have and the challenges we either face up to or capitulate, and accept dependence and reliance on others.

This story is not simply one of fortitude, however, of overcoming disability in the most amazing way, but of a truly historic character – someone like Nicholas Saunderson, that the world really does need to hear about, to marvel at and to celebrate.

But it isn't the much-travelled horseman (in advance of Guide Dogs for the Blind), nor the chancer, the businessman trading in anything worth trading in, which really catches my attention. Not even the musician with Cumberland's army, leading up to Culloden. Rather it is the astonishing feats of John Metcalf as road builder.

We can imagine that he knew all too well the pitfalls of the most appalling roads imaginable. When he had the opportunity to act as contractor and overseer, he did something about it – taking up the challenge from the Turnpike Acts, and creating mile after mile of durable and useable road, opening up not only the social life but the commerce of each area.

My lasting impression is of someone who was both inspirational and, I imagine, infuriating. Nevertheless, he commanded the friendship and patronage of some of the wealthiest people in Yorkshire and beyond, travelling to London and Scotland on foot, on horseback, sometimes by sea. He seemed to find a way to fit in and take on every obstacle as though it were just another stride along one of the once-impassable roads.

If, as a small boy, I had known about this eighteenth-century Yorkshireman, blinded by disease, perhaps I would have been daunted in attempting to follow in his footsteps. But I did not – and now that through this book I have come to know him, I can rejoice in his example and inspiration.

Author's Preface

Although John Metcalf, known to the world as Blind Jack, died in 1810, this is the first comprehensive biography of him – in the sense that it ranges over the whole field of available material and draws together many loose and scattered ends. The reason for this long delay in doing him justice is that the public have had access to Blind Jack's own account of his life – the memoirs he dictated in 1795 reprinted without notes or comment many times since. Apart from a semi-fictionalised version by Gary Hogg (1967) and a novel based on part of his life by Alan Plowright (2002) – neither of these free from mistakes and historical improbabilities – there has been no attempt at a definitive study based both on local knowledge and extensive research.

Blind Jack's original personal account still remains an essential framework, of course. But it cannot be taken just as it stands. In the first place, it is obviously ghost-written and presented in educated English – whereas Blind Jack, like all working Yorkshiremen of his day, spoke in down-to-earth dialect (specifically North Riding dialect), a few fragments of which I have been able to retrieve. Then we have to watch out for possible lapses of memory (he was then nearly seventy-eight), and the confusions, misunderstandings or alterations made by the amanuensis to whom he was telling his story. Most of all, we have to ask whether Jack himself is giving us the plain facts or adding colour and spin – as though he imagined he was telling tales to his cronies in the alehouse or impressing the ladies and gentlemen visiting Harrogate Spa.

So, far from taking his narrative at face value, I have used it as a kind of skeleton, which I have fleshed out wherever possible by research into the eighteenth-century context, spending many happy hours trawling through libraries and archives. I have also visited most of the places where Blind Jack worked – and in particular made use of my familiarity with Yorkshire, and especially Knaresborough. I have certainly not been lacking in a conducive atmosphere, and have been able to show people Blind Jack's haunts, take them along his roads, and give talks about him in the very places in Harrogate and Knaresborough where he played his fiddle.

Long years ago I came to teach at Harrogate (Ashville College), then moved to Knaresborough (King James's School). My enthusiasm for local history led to such digressions in class that many former pupils tell me they remember more about Knaresborough's remarkable characters than they do about what I was supposed to be teaching them! Of all these local characters, it is Blind Jack who stands head and shoulders above the rest – indeed, who boldly steps out with his stick into the wider world, a unique and arresting figure of national and even international interest.

Ours is the age of the cult of celebrity. One after the other, special achievers are singled out for extravagant admiration and even idolization. Well, here is one you might have missed. Commenting on a list of 'The Top Ten Greatest Disabled Britons' published in 2006, Peter White, BBC Disability Affairs Correspondent, asked 'Where is Blind Jack of Knaresborough? Not much historical perspective here!' So this book seeks to give a worthy celebrity his rightful recognition. I am confident that, once he is known, he will not be forgotten.

Chapter One

Birthplace and Early Childhood

John Metcalf opens the account of his life, issued in 1795, with the statement that he 'was born at Knaresborough on the 15 of August, 1717'.[1] No record of his baptism appears in the Knaresborough Parish Register, but this date is confirmed by the portrait in his memoirs dated 31 August 1795, stating him to be 'Aged 78', and by the inscription on his gravestone in the churchyard of All Saints', Spofforth: 'He died on the 26th April, 1810 in the 93rd year of his age.' A clear enough sentence, but one often misquoted in those accounts which state that he was actually ninety-three when he died, rather than ninety-two.

What sort of place was the Knaresborough into which this Metcalf child was born? In the early years of the eighteenth century it was a small market town in what was then the northern part of the West Riding of Yorkshire, situated 3 miles to the north-east of Harrogate. Though its population by the end of the century had only reached 4,000 or so, Knaresborough was a town with some status, priding itself on its past, and still returning two MPs to Parliament. It had seen many upheavals and felt the effects of the Civil War, but the general political background was now comparatively stable. In 1714 George I had come to the throne, and though this Hanoverian monarch himself made little impact, his choice of Sir Robert Walpole as the first British Prime Minister was to benefit the country greatly.

There would be a few of the very oldest inhabitants who had been alive in the days when Knaresborough Castle was still intact – an extensive royal residence, which had originated in what the Angles called *Knarresburg*, 'the fortress on the rock'. It had later been developed as a Norman castle, visited by the Kings and Queens of England, notably King John, who enjoyed hunting in the royal forest of Knaresborough, and who presented the first known Royal Maundy here in 1210. Then there was Edward I, and Edward II, who had granted Knaresborough a Charter in 1310, and who for Piers Gaveston rebuilt the castle, giving it a dozen towers and a great keep. He was followed by Edward III and Queen Philippa, by their son, John of Gaunt, Duke of Lancaster – and Richard II was held here briefly as a prisoner.

In its splendid position, some 120ft above the River Nidd, dominating its fairytale wooded gorge, the castle must have seemed impregnable. But on 20 December 1644 it had been taken by Parliamentarians, still flushed with their famous July victory at Marston Moor. Four years later, following the decree of Parliament, it was, like other Royalist castles, systematically 'slighted' – made untenable, and largely dismantled, stone by stone, with gunpowder, pick and crowbar. No doubt when Cromwell stayed here – in 1648, when he saw the work in progress – he perhaps admired the magnificent view that even he could not destroy.

Though the town had in general been loyal to Charles I, once the castle was demolished the good folk of Knaresborough were only too ready to make use of the quality stone, ready-cut, which partly explains why so many of the older houses are built of this honey-coloured locally quarried magnesian limestone. The loss of the castle would to some extent have had an effect on the town's economy. No longer would there be a garrison to be supplied with provisions and material. Indeed, it could be argued that it was the very existence of the early fortress that had given rise to a community to supply its needs, with a market place that originally extended as far as the gates of the castle.

The eighteenth-century setting of Blind Jack's birthplace.

The market itself, however, was strong enough to withstand the loss of a military presence. In Tudor times it had been noted by Henry VIII's antiquary, John Leland, that 'the market there is quick' (lively). Over the years it sold all kinds of produce from the local farms and orchards, including liquorice and cherries, for which it was once well known. A few years before Blind Jack's birth the town celebrated its growing prosperity by erecting in 1709 a new market cross, the base of which can still be seen, surrounded by a token remnant of the cobbles that once surfaced the whole market place. During the course of Jack's life the market seems to have gone from strength to strength. The year before he died the remarkable statement was made by Ely Hargrove that 'the quantity of corn sold here every week is supposed to exceed that of any other market in the county'.[2]

As well as Knaresborough acting as the hub of an extensive area of farming, its economy also depended upon the growing spa trade at nearby Harrogate, and a considerable cottage industry in cloth. Textile workers, including weavers or 'websters', dyers and fullers, are mentioned in documents here from as early as the fourteenth century. Sometimes a farmer would spin and weave the wool from his sheep, grow hemp to be turned into the coarse cloth known as 'harden', and flax to be turned into linen. The latter was especially common in Knaresborough, and by 1700 inventories show that there were thirty-one weavers and forty-eight looms in Knaresborough and Scriven, in a growing cottage industry producing mainly linen, which was dyed and finished locally.[3]

The fields round Knaresborough were once mainly blue with flax, but it was increasingly being imported through Hull from the Baltic – 500 tons of it, for example, in 1717, the year of Blind Jack's birth. By the 1780s Knaresborough was producing a thousand pieces of linen a week, each 20 yards by 35in.[4] By this time the scattered workers in farms and cottages were being organised by companies such as Walton's, founded in 1785, who took over Castle Mill, situated on the Nidd, with its own weir and water power. This had started as a paper-mill in 1770, was rebuilt as a cotton mill in 1791, but was adapted by Walton's, eventually producing linen of such quality that it supplied all Queen Victoria's royal household. In the early years of the eighteenth century, however, linen was still Knaresborough's essential cottage industry, and the Metcalf family may well have been connected with it in some way.

Blind Jack's parents are described in his published memoirs as 'working people'. They lived in the centre of the town, near the lower end of High Street, and whereas Jack's mother could have worked as a linen weaver, for example, the father appears to have had some connection with the farms, and perhaps been a carrier or horsebreeder, if we interpret the terse statement that he 'kept horses'. His son also tells us that as a disciplinarian his father was 'rather severe', but he seems to have been a good parent and always encouraged Jack to make the most of himself.

Certainly, John Metcalf was not born into abject poverty – an assumption sometimes made by writers who have imagined a rise from rags to riches. It is true that he encouraged the notion of a humble origin when he wrote (in wording surely supplied by his publishers) in the dedication of the second edition of his memoirs (1801):

> ...although my low and obscure station of life, in great measure, precluded me from such opportunities of society and conversation as tend to polish and refine men's minds and feelings... I have never ceased to be conscious of the obligation I am under to my friends and benefactors.[5]

He might have added that he was under even greater obligation to his parents, who managed to send him to a small private school, and pay for him to have music lessons. The Metcalfs, though by no means wealthy, seem to have been in good standing in the town, and had connections, for example, with the master of a local pack of hounds, named Woodburn, who befriended and encouraged young Metcalf.

Where in Knaresborough is Blind Jack's birthplace? His home would certainly have been a tourist draw if it had existed today but it was demolished during his lifetime and the best we can do is describe its probable location. This was established by Thomas Sutcliffe of Leeds in about 1860 when he made a special visit to Knaresborough one market day, and went round asking the locals what they knew about where Metcalf was born. He recorded that they could only tell him that he would 'larn all aboot 'im fra t toon-crier, who was an auld man an' knew ivverybody'. The town crier was no help, but Sutcliffe was eventually directed to the ninety-year-old retired pharmacist, Michael Calvert, author of the little *History of Knaresborough*, which in 1844 had taken its place alongside the various editions of Hargrove's history.

Calvert told Sutcliffe that John Metcalf was born in a house which once stood to the east of the parish church, and that 'Jack's garden and croft came down as far as the churchyard'.[6] This was presumably on land owned by the Collins family because when their home, Knaresborough House, was built in about 1768 the Metcalf home was demolished. To understand why, we need to see the Collins house today. Attributed to the famous York architect, John Carr, it was built as the home of James Collins and also associated with his uncle, the Revd Thomas Collins, who served as Knaresborough's longest-serving vicar from 1735 to 1788.[7] Facing the bottom of High Street, it is a fine Georgian building, and now an appropriate home for Knaresborough Town Council. It enjoys a spacious setting, and from the terrace at the rear there was a delightful view – before the trees obscured part of it – of the parish church. As we look towards the church we can see where the wall separates the grounds of Knaresborough House from the churchyard. It was somewhere here, to our left, that the Metcalf cottage stood, and was perhaps removed to improve the view when the grounds were landscaped.

On the strength of what Calvert had told him, Sutcliffe decided he would climb to the top of the church tower. Looking east, he says, 'I sketched, designed and filled up, from the description given to me, the view of Blind Jack's birthplace'. As there was nothing left of it we can take it that this sketch was his own idea of what it might have looked like – a one-storey thatched cottage or small house – situated somewhere down there, a little to his left, with the end of King James's Grammar School (built 1616, but rebuilt on the same site in 1741) seen over to the right.[8] An eighteenth-century engraving shows the thatched vicarage and workhouse (built 1737), with a glimpse of what is said to have been the Metcalf home (in this case a small house of more than one storey) beyond the east end of the parish church.[9]

John Metcalf, presumably known as 'Jack' from an early age, must have been seen by his parents as an intelligent child with potential. He tells us that at the age of four he 'was put to school by his parents'. This would have been some small dame school where the little boy would be taught to read, write and 'cypher', as arithmetic was then often called. The small King James's Grammar School, popularly known as 'the Free School', was almost next door to the Metcalf home and it is conceivable that he received some elementary education there as one of the 'petties', perhaps in later years. But he makes no mention of this, and his contact with the nearby school may have been limited to his hearing the boys at play, speaking to each other only in Latin – if they still followed the original school rules of 1616.

It was fortunate that Jack started school as early as the age of four, and had two years of instruction and increasing familiarity with written words and numbers before he was struck by catastrophe. This is described in his memoirs by the laconic statement: 'He continued at school two years. He was then seized with the small-pox which rendered him totally blind.'[10]

Early editions of Hargrove unfortunately confuse the age he started school with the age he contracted the disease and erroneously state that 'he lost his sight when only four years old'.[11] This is a mistake which has been copied many times. The age is important. Those two years of schooling as a normally-sighted child were vital in giving him a better start, as he learnt to adapt to his world of darkness. It would obviously have been so much harder for him if he had been blinded at four, or in early infancy. He had, in fact, an advantage over Nicholas Saunderson, the brilliant Yorkshire mathematician who ended up as a successor to Newton at Cambridge. He had been blinded by smallpox when aged only one, and 'lost his sight so early in infancy that he did not remember to have ever seen'.[12]

The eighteenth-century term 'the small-pox', with the hyphen, is significant. It was then still regarded as a close cousin of the even more virulent disease of 'the great-pox' or syphilis – sometimes called 'French' or 'Spanish pox'. Second only to the plagues of earlier centuries, smallpox was a terrifying scourge, a rapidly spreading infection which either killed its victims or marked for life those it could not kill. Disfigured people, described as 'pock-marked', were a common enough sight in Knaresborough, as everywhere else. For a contemporary example we need look no further than the case of Eugene Aram, the Knaresborough schoolmaster hanged in 1759 for the murder (in 1744) of the shoemaker, Daniel Clark – both men likely to have been known to John Metcalf. Not only had Aram himself survived a serious attack of smallpox as a young man (then working in London), but when his victim went missing – at first presumed to have absconded with defrauded valuables – he was advertised in the York Courant as 'a thin, pale-looking Pock-broke Man'.[13] About four years older than Metcalf, it is possible that Clark was infected as a child during the same epidemic.

The first comment we might make about the smallpox attack on the Metcalf child is that, at the age of six, he must have had a strong constitution to be able to survive the ravages of this appalling disease – the cause in the eighteenth century of nearly half-a-million deaths each year in Europe, about 10 per cent of all deaths in England, and up to 35 per cent of deaths in children. Jack's parents must have feared the worst as they watched over their boy lying there tormented by this virus-induced disease, known to doctors by its Latin name of *variola*. The symptoms included a raging fever, headache, delirium and convulsions. Then – three or four days after the onset of the fever – a rash of red spots would appear, usually starting on the face and quickly spreading all over the body. After a day or so the spots would become painful pustules, giving the skin a loathsome and alarming appearance.

Could any treatment have been given? None at all for smallpox – and the only way to combat this disease was a system developed in the east known as 'inoculation' or 'variolation'. This meant the deliberate infection of a healthy person by rubbing pus from a smallpox patient into a cut, and hoping that the healthy person would develop a mild form of smallpox, and then be immune to further infection. In 1717 – the very year of Blind Jack's birth – the wife of the British Ambassador to Turkey, then living in Constantinople, was in the news because she had her young son treated in this way, starting a fashion which spread through Europe.[14]

This early form of inoculation, using the actual virus, often worked, but it could also prove fatal. This is why Dr Edward Jenner, who regularly practised variolation, looked for a safer method. He eventually found it, when he noticed that milkmaids who had picked up cowpox never seemed to contact smallpox. The great turning point came when he introduced cowpox material into two cuts in the arm of an eight-year-old boy, James Phipps, in Berkeley, Gloucestershire. This was the first official 'vaccination' (from the Latin *vacca*, meaning 'cow'), later the means of saving countless millions of lives. But this first vaccination did not take place until 1796, far too late for the six-year-old Knaresborough patient in 1723.

Some local doctor may well have been called in by the Metcalfs. Physicians were increasingly likely to be available because of their interest in making money out of those taking the waters at the nearby spa wells.[15] Medicines, at least, were available from the apothecary's in Knaresborough market place, where we can still see the Oldest Chemist's Shop, in use as a pharmacy from at least 1720. There John Beckwith dispensed all kinds of pills and potions, mostly herbal remedies. He could no doubt have made up some concoction, including an infusion of Peruvian Bark, for example, which might have helped to reduce the fever, and also supplied an ointment to soothe the inflamed skin. But such things were only palliative, and all the folk remedies were mere superstition. In John Wesley's curious collection of such remedies, published in 1747, smallpox patients were to be given diluted milk, lots of cold water, and fed on lentils and rape seed, 'a certain cure for small-pox'.[16]

By the second week of the disease, scabs were forming over the pustules, and about three weeks later these started to fall off, revealing, in many cases, the characteristic legacy of pock-marking. There is, incidentally, no mention of Blind Jack having been left pock-marked, and no sign of it in the one authentic portrait we have of him. By this time Jack would be beginning to feel well again, but the infection had spread to his eyes, with a disastrous result. This was the severe inflammation of the cornea (the whole transparent front of the eye), known to doctors as keratitis. Severe infection of the delicate and sensitive cornea and conjunctiva invariably produced deep ulceration and scarring – and an opaque filming over that could mean complete blindness.[17]

The adult Metcalf retained some vague memory of the concern of his parents when his inability to see was first noticed. 'All possible means', he tells us, 'were used to preserve his sight.' A pair of ancient spectacles was once presented to the town council by someone who thought these might have been used to try to help Blind Jack, but the date of these shows that this is unlikely.[18] The irony is that Jack's retina would have remained intact, and that in modern times a corneal transplant might have restored his vision perfectly. Yet the disease left him blind in both eyes for the rest of his long life.

This leads to the second comment to be made about the smallpox attack. The crucial question which many have asked – in view of the astonishing range of things that John Metcalf did – is simply this: was he completely blind? Though the smallpox had damaged his eyes, did it not leave him with at least partial sight? The answer to this question is, firstly, that smallpox was a well-known cause of blindness in the eighteenth century, when it was responsible for about a third of all cases of total loss of sight. Secondly, there is not a hint in any of the contemporary literature that anybody suspected that he was able to see just a little. Records of astonishment at his exploits are all in the context of the acceptance that he was completely blind. In one anecdote there is even a reference to the damaged cornea, when the bleariness of his eyes is at first assumed to be the result of heavy drinking.[19]

It is true that the statement that the smallpox 'rendered him totally blind'[20] as well as the account of his astonishing activities, are mainly derived from his own memoirs. But as these were first published in 1795 – about fifteen years before he died – there was plenty of opportunity for his claims to be challenged. Apparently they never were, and although we might concede that John Metcalf could perhaps have perceived the difference between bright sunlight and total darkness, there is every reason to accept that he was indeed accurately nicknamed 'Blind Jack'.

The energetic determination which was typical of his whole life is first seen in the way he bounced back after his devastating childhood illness. He tells us that 'about six months after recovering from the small-pox' he was able, without anyone guiding him, to walk from his home to the end of the street – presumably a short street leading to the bottom of High Street – and then find his way back. Three years later, he says, he was able to find his way to any part of Knaresborough.

Early signs of his sociable and gregarious nature are seen in his determination not to allow his blindness to isolate him from other children and normal play. Blind Jack wanted to grow up like any other boy of his age, not confined to idleness indoors, but enjoying life out in the fresh air. Speaking of himself, he tells us that soon he had:

> ...begun to associate with boys of his own age, going with them to seek birds nests, and for his share of the eggs and young birds he was able to climb in trees, while his comrades waited at the bottom to direct him to the nests and to receive what he should throw down... He would now ramble into the lanes and fields alone, to the distance of two or three miles, and return.[21]

In these words we can detect the beginnings of the vagabond life that would later become so typical of him. Even as a child he had learnt to appreciate the sense of freedom that comes from being out in the open, wandering along the lanes and across the fields all by himself – not with the faltering steps of a blind boy, escorted by a guide, or hesitatingly feeling his way, but with the confident stride of a lad who has made up his mind he will not be beaten.

Chapter Two

From Teenage Escapades to Spa Musician

The adjustment and rehabilitation made by young Blind Jack was not without encouragement and support. First, there would be help from his parents, brothers and sisters. We do not have any details concerning his siblings, but there is a reference in the memoirs to 'other children'. There would be other relations, too, and helpful friends and neighbours.

In addition, the family would be visited by the vicar of Knaresborough, at this time the Revd Joshua Glover, incumbent from 1716 to 1735. Both his church and the vicarage were very close to the Metcalf home, and he may well have helped Jack to resume the education that had been disrupted when he was six. Glover certainly knew how precious young life was. The year before Jack's illness he had lost his own firstborn son at the age of four years and four months.[1] Could this also have been from smallpox?

As the churchyard, well stocked with tombs and headstones, was just over the wall from Jack's garden, it is not too fanciful to suggest that – whether the vicar was involved or not – the blind boy was encouraged to keep up his ability to read by running his fingers over the inscriptions incised on the gravestones. This is, in fact, how his near-contemporary fellow-victim of smallpox, Nicholas Saunderson, had himself learnt to read.

Systems for helping the blind to read were then sporadic and rudimentary. It was not until 1784 that the first schools for the blind were founded in Paris, introducing embossed books in which the letters were raised on thick paper, rather than cut into stone. It was not until 1829 that Louis Braille published his more efficient alphabet based on a system of dots.

Tactile impressions, and the development of exquisitely sensitive fingertips, are obviously essential for the blind from the very beginning. Many later instances show how John Metcalf was essentially a man who felt his way through life, habitually experiencing the world through a highly developed sense of touch that could, for example, distinguish the shapes and figures slightly embossed on playing cards.

As in the case of blind people throughout history, his sense of hearing also showed a marked compensatory development, and he became fully alive to the world of sound. Like so many others in his condition he was led to make the most of music, and at the age of thirteen he started lessons, learning to play the violin, and later the haut-bois or oboe. From the start he showed real talent, but his dislike of having to stay indoors to practice, rather than being out in the fresh air and in the countryside, is indicated by the comment: '...he had conceived more taste for the cry of a hound or harrier than the sound of any instrument.'[2]

This specifically refers to a passion for hunting which had been aroused in him by Mr Woodburn, master of a local pack of hounds. This could have been William Woodburn, whose daughter, Mary, married the Revd Thomas Collins in 1734.[3] A 'William Woodburne, gentleman' is also mentioned in Knaresborough wills at this time. Just to please this blind lad Woodburn started to take him along with him when he went hunting, and soon became very fond of his company. Because Jack's father kept horses, he had already learnt to ride well, and showed no fear even when galloping. Now he added to his expertise with horses an interest in hunting-dogs, owning three of them himself. One of his earliest recorded pieces of mischief is the reminiscence that in spring he used to slip out between ten and eleven o'clock at night and take his hounds for a run, along with some of Woodburn's. This, he says, was partly because he so enjoyed the cry of the hounds and also so they could catch a few hares. On one occasion a young hound attacked and worried a couple of lambs, and this meant he had to discontinue his nightly escapades.[4]

In his seventy-eighth year, when he was dictating his life story, he exhibited that facility, so common in older people, of vivid recollection of the early days. Old Metcalf relived with relish the exploits of his teenage years – exploits which, in modern times, would have meant he would have been in trouble with the authorities, including the police.

This was not through lack of discipline at home, as is shown by a story he tells of an incident at the age of fourteen. Strong and agile, he had a particular fondness for climbing trees, and one Sunday he went with his pals to pick the plums from a tree on the site of a ruined farmhouse near Knaresborough, still privately owned. While he was busy picking the plums and dropping them down for his companions to collect, the owner appeared, and the gang fled, leaving Jack – unable to hear what was happening because of the noise of a high wind – still stuck up the tree. As soon as he understood the situation, he clambered down so quickly that he missed his footing and fell headlong into a gravel pit. At that side of the tree, he remembered, he was on land belonging to Sir Harry Slingsby, which added further trespass to his theft.

The fall left him stunned and breathless, and had cut a large gash across his face. He recalls how he was almost too frightened to go home in case his strict father should see his injury and find out what he had been up to.[5] As a typical teenager, he made sure that most of his misdemeanours were unknown to his parents, who seem to have trusted him and allowed him considerable freedom, rightly believing that their blind boy should grow up as normal as possible, mixing with other lively lads of his age. Unless he slipped out unnoticed, they even seem to have allowed him to be out late at night – possibly thinking that his blindness meant that the hours of darkness would mean no difference to his ability to get around.

So young Metcalf, day and night, led an outdoor life, exploring the town and surrounding countryside with his fellow teenagers, handling horses and dogs, climbing trees and, every autumn, specialising in stealing fruit. From the amateurish theft of a few plums the gang of boys had now graduated to carefully planned raids on orchards, all organised by Blind Jack. Tall, with a commanding personality, and no doubt more daring than the rest, he had clearly taken over as leader.

The Metcalf gang found an ideal den in the porch of the parish church, the main part of which was always locked at night. The porch, added in the early sixteenth century, with a fanlight grill added in Blind Jack's day, and with a long seat down each side, would make the perfect meeting place for a teenage gang.

One night they assembled there as usual, between eleven o'clock and midnight. Having discussed how they would set about stealing apples from a nearby orchard, they successfully carried out their theft, then returned to the porch to share out the booty. In a jolly mood, one of the lads decided he would pretend they were going to celebrate by having a drink at an alehouse. He lifted up the large iron ring which normally opened the door of the church, now locked, and gave it a loud rap. Then he shouted out: 'A tankard of ale here!'

Immediately a very loud voice from inside the church shouted back: 'You are at the wrong house!' The lads were too shocked and scared to move. Then Jack asked: 'Did you not hear summat speak in t' church?'

Whether this something was a man or ghost, the experience was so terrifying that the lads suddenly took to their heels, running from the porch, and out of the churchyard. Jack, unaffected by the darkness, ran 'as fast as any of them.'

After a whispered discussion they plucked up courage and went down the flagged pathway back to the church. To their astonishment it now looked as if the building they thought locked and empty was on fire, with lights blazing in the windows. They entered the porch again, but before they could reach the door the latch was noisily rattled from inside. Off they ran a second time, 'terrified and speechless'.[6]

A member of the gang by the name of Clemishaw ran home and was in such a desperate fright that he got into bed with his mother. His father was absent – for an unusual reason. Clemishaw senior was the Knaresborough sexton, and had been called out by the vicar to make a kind of secret burial. An old lady, wife of the Revd Dr Talbot, former vicar of Spofforth, had died, and her body had been brought for burial inside Knaresborough parish church.[7] Because some of the relations lived at a distance, the funeral had been delayed, and the body was now beginning to decompose and smell. Complaints about this led the vicar to order a hasty burial at dead of night – and the great number of candles he had lit to illuminate his macabre task had been mistaken by the boys for a fire.[8]

The River Nidd flowing through Knaresborough was in certain places ideal for swimming, particularly in the deeper part above High Bridge. By the age of fourteen Blind Jack was an excellent swimmer, so skilful and vigorous that he became a terror to the older boys swimming with him, because of his trick of seizing them from underneath, then dragging them to the bottom. He swam in other rivers, too, and had the reputation of being a keen angler. When he was older he once swam in the deepest part of the Wharfe for three hours, catching fish by holding the strings of the net in his mouth, so he could swim with both hands free.[9]

As he was accustomed to groping his way in permanent darkness, Jack found it easier than a sighted swimmer to explore the murky depths. So he became adept at recovering what was well below the surface, especially in his local river, the Nidd. On one occasion a soldier had drowned, thought to have been 'taken with the cramp' – probably in the still-notorious Cherry Tree Deep. Jack had to dive in four times before he managed to find the soldier's body.[10] His reputation as a diver meant that by the age of fifteen he was being employed to recover from the river items such as valuable pieces of timber which had been carried along when the Nidd was in flood, and had lodged in the mud of the deepest parts.

In 1732 a man called John Barker, who kept the inn just to the west of High Bridge, also participated in Knaresborough's linen industry, bleaching yarn and weaving his own cloth.[11] One day he was making use of the adjacent river to wash two bales of yarn, when a violent rainstorm caused the current to swell so rapidly that his yarn was suddenly swept away, carried under High Bridge, and then sank in the depths at the other side. Young Metcalf happened to call at the inn a few days later. He knew Barker well (indeed, he seemed to know all the innkeepers) and immediately offered to recover the bales for him. He procured some long cart-ropes, fastened hooks to the end and got friends standing on the bridge to hold the other ends. Then he dived into the river – at this point said to be about 21ft deep – attached the ropes to the bales of yarn and then called for them to be pulled by his friends clear of the water. This was another early example of Blind Jack's determination to overcome difficulties, and of his ingenuity in solving practical problems.[12]

Not long after this incident Jack helped out another friend. He was drinking late at night at another inn, this time in the adjacent hamlet of Scriven, when he heard two men arguing about some stray sheep that had been put into the pound or pinfold. One was Jack's friend, Robert Scaif, the owner of the sheep, and he claimed he had been unjustly treated.

Deciding he could soon sort this matter out, Jack bade his drinking friends goodnight, went out in the pitch darkness to the pinfold, climbed over the wall, and – one by one – grabbed the imprisoned sheep and lifted them over the wall, restoring their freedom.[13]

As a frequenter of the Knaresborough inns, Jack soon became interested in the cock pits that were attached to several of them. With the help of his friends he began to attend cockfights and take part in the gambling, sitting as close as possible to the action, with his friends advising him, by discreet touches, how he should place his bets. He kept his own game birds and exercised them at a cock-walk in his garden. Such was his enthusiasm that he constantly sought to improve his stock, and claimed that 'if at any time he heard of a better game cock than his own he was sure to get him by some means or other, though at a hundred miles distance'.

At one cockfight a rival unfairly armed his bird with a steel spur, so that it defeated Metcalf's champion. As an outrageous act of revenge for this, Blind Jack got a friend to help him – once again at dead of night – to seal all the windows of his rival's house with cabbage leaves, skewered together. This meant that he and his family would not realise when daylight had returned. When they eventually got up they found they were prisoners in their own home, because the door had been walled up with mud and stones, and the floor of the house flooded. On this occasion, knowing who the culprit was, the victim reported him to the local justice, who issued a warrant for Metcalf's arrest. But, as no proof could be found, the case was dismissed.[14]

Although Blind Jack now had a reputation for ingenious mischief making and was suspected every time there was any crime or vandalism, he always managed to elude detection. His reputation extended well beyond Knaresborough, as in the case of the large rookery his gang raided at Bilton, 2 miles away. The taking of rooks was not ordinary cruelty or vandalism, but theft that could be profitable, because the birds were then commonly eaten in pies. The Metcalf gang made several attempts to get at the rookery, but were driven off each time by the owner of the land. So Jack got one of his lads to give him a careful account of the position of the nests, then went with them late at night, climbed up to the positions he had memorised and brought down the birds. They killed them, and took away 'seven dozen and a half, excepting the heads, which they left under the trees.[15] When the owner saw the heads of his decapitated rooks the next day, he sent the town crier round the district with an offer of two guineas for information. Once again, though, the young nocturnal malefactor was never brought to justice.

To balance these near-criminal activities there were instances of real helpfulness, as in the case of recovery work on the river, or the instance of how he helped another friend who had lost a key and locked himself out. With some pride old Metcalf recalled how he climbed up the thatched roof and let himself down the chimney – only to get stuck because it was too narrow. So, with typical resourcefulness, he struggled back to the top, took off all his clothes and managed to squeeze himself down the chimney so he could open the door from the inside. He recalls that his clothes, left on the roof, were soaked by a sudden shower, and that he had to wait until they dried before he could climb up, stark naked, to recover them.[16]

This kind of story would help to redeem Blind Jack in the eyes of the Knaresborough gossips who were saying that he would come to no good. Another thing in his favour was his growing reputation as a violinist. Having started lessons at the age of thirteen, he had, within a year or so, made such progress that he was able to go round playing at county dances, and also at a fortnightly public dance held in Knaresborough. In the Christmas season he joined three other players to go round as waits, playing carols and festive tunes in the open air.

The Queen's Head, High Harrogate.

His reputation as a fiddler, as well as a lively personality, brought him an invitation, at the age of fifteen, to become the official musician at the nearby spa:

In the year 1732 Metcalf was invited to Harrogate to succeed, as fiddler, a poor old man who had played there for 70 years, and who, being borne down by the weight of 100 years, began to play too slow for country dancing. The old man died in the 102nd year of his age, and played in the summer season the year he died.[17]

The old fiddler was a character called Morrison, often referred to by visitors to the spa. There could scarcely have been a greater contrast than that between this veteran violinist and the vivacious teenager who replaced him.

The inn where he succeeded Morrison as violinist was the Queen's Head. This was Harrogate's oldest inn, dating from soon after 1660, when it was presumably named after Queen Catherine, wife of the newly restored Charles II.[18] Although it was largely rebuilt in 1855, certain features have been retained, and, in what is now the Cedar Court Hotel, the large assembly room with its musicians gallery gives some idea of what it might have been like in Blind Jack's day. Moreover, his ghostly footsteps, I have been told by hotel staff, can still be heard along the corridors.

The Queen's Head was in the village of High Harrogate. It looked across the spacious green of the Stray, where, over to the right, you could see the Tewit Well. This was the first of the mineral springs to be discovered, when in about 1571 William Slingsby realised the water had similar properties to those he had tasted at Spa in Belgium. By 1626 it was being promoted by the York physician, Edmund Deane, as 'The English Spaw Fountaine' in a book, *Spadacrene Anglica*, whose first chapter gave fulsome praise to Knaresborough. This historic town was seen by Dr Deane as the ideal place to stay for health seekers visiting the various wells some 3 miles away, such as the Tewit Well and the Old Sulphur Well, the latter aptly nicknamed 'The Stinking Spaw'.

Because there was at first so little accommodation near the wells, Knaresborough became the acknowledged base for visitors, and throughout the seventeenth century was known as 'The Knaresborough Spa'.[19] Even by the end of the century travellers like Celia Fiennes chose to stay in Knaresborough when visiting the wells, and, if we refer again to the year of Blind Jack's birth, 1717 was the year in which Daniel Defoe stayed in Knaresborough. There he saw the Dropping Well and its petrifactions, then went out to see the Harrogate wells, finding 'a great deal of good company here drinking the Waters'. This surprised Defoe, because it seemed 'a most desolate out-of-the-world place'.[20]

By 1732, however, there were two growing villages offering purpose-built accommodation and other facilities near the wells: High Harrogate, within sight of the Tewit Well and close to St John's Well, and Low Harrogate, which was centred on the Old Sulphur Well. By 1821, when the population of Knaresborough was 5,283, that of High Harrogate was 1,583 and Low Harrogate 1,010. High Harrogate, which Blind Jack knew best, was the more populous and prosperous of the two, and because it was within the Parish of Knaresborough, the vicar, the Revd Thomas Collins, started a public subscription list which led to the building of St John's Chapel of Ease in 1749, replaced in 1831 by Christ Church. By the end of the nineteenth century the two Harrogate villages had coalesced to become a flourishing town of about 30,000, while Knaresborough remained static.[21]

These figures, of course, are of residents, and the number would be increased by many thousands if we included the summer influx of visitors who flocked 'in the season' to drink the health-giving waters and enjoy the spa experience that was fast becoming a feature of European society in general, and England in particular.

So Blind Jack, plunged into the midst of the fashionable world of spa visitors, was not only now in gainful employment, but perfectly placed to make the most of contacts with the rich and influential people who congregated at the Queen's Head. This fifteen-year-old fiddler was not going to live out his life like his predecessor, fiddling away for seventy years, entertaining his superiors. He realised that if he played his cards well his appointment as spa musician could have far-reaching consequences. He would profit from acquaintance with members of the landed gentry and other high-placed people, and through them gain admittance to a wider world of varied and fulfilling activities.

Chapter Three

Taking the Waters: Huntsman, Guide, Bon Vivant

Blind Jack started work at the spa during an especially interesting period of its development. Already the economic centre of gravity was beginning to shift from Knaresborough to Harrogate, which was increasingly being seen, with its new accommodation, as a spa in its own right. Though visitors still continued to stay in Knaresborough, there was far less of what had been described in the seventeenth century as 'the great resort to it in summer by reason of the wells.'[1]

Growing enthusiasm for spa treatment was part of a national trend. Writing in 1734, Dr Thomas Short noted over 200 spas in England, from Bath and Cheltenham to obscure springs and wells. 'One would think the English were ducks,' observed Horace Walpole, 'They are for ever waddling to the waters.' They certainly waddled to the waters of Harrogate, where they expected to find, along with good inns and hydrotherapy, an agreeable social life, including the regular dances which now largely depended on young Metcalf's direction.

The ladies and gentlemen who came to the spa did not usually over-exert themselves. Their most strenuous activity was to 'rise early and repair to the wells'.[2] These were, firstly, the Tewit Well, and the much-nearer Old Spaw or St John's Well. Here they drank the pleasant-tasting chalybeate water, containing mainly iron salts, helpful for anaemia, for example. Secondly, they could go further, down to Low Harrogate, and visit the Old Sulphur Well. Here they could face the ordeal of drinking the sulphur water, stinking with the noxious fumes of hydrogen sulphide, which produced what came to be known as the 'Harrogate headache'. Some doctors were cheerfully recommending patients drink up to five or six pints of this nauseating brew from the bowels of the earth. Such patients must have been phenomenally constipated, because one sure effect of this sulphur water was a drastic purge. Safer, and less disgusting, was bathing in the water, especially when it had been warmed – an effective remedy, it was found, for skin diseases.

One of the most amusing accounts of life at the spa is found in Tobias Smollett's epistolary novel, *Humphry Clinker*. Although it is based on the author's experiences in Harrogate in 1766, by which time Blind Jack was no longer permanently based there, it gives an interesting picture of the context in which the young musician found himself. It describes how each of the inns formed a distinct society. One inn, he says, was 'already full up to the very garrets, having no less than fifty lodgers and as many servants.' Yet he found in the crowds of health seekers a company 'far more agreeable than one could expect from an accidental assemblage of persons, who are utter strangers to one another.'[3]

However, in the guise of another of his letter writers, Smollet, who was a qualified physician, grumbles about the bleak landscape, overcrowded inns, and the horror of drinking the sulphur water that smelled of 'rotten eggs':

> I was obliged to hold my nose with one hand, while I advanced the glass to my mouth with the other; and after I had made shift to swallow it, my stomach could hardly retain what it had received. The only effects it produced were sickness, griping, and insurmountable disgust. I can hardly mention it without puking. The world is strangely misled by the affectation of singularity. I cannot help suspecting that this water owes its reputation in a great measure to its being so strikingly offensive.[4]

Although Smollet refers to visitors riding in their own carriages to the wells, an important part of 'the cure' was taking exercise, and resident doctors always recommended plenty of walking. For this reason Hargrove gives, in the first edition of *History* (1775), a list showing the walking distances from Blind Jack's base of the Queen's Head to the various wells, starting with the four other principal inns. It is worth quoting this in full, as it gives a good idea of the topography with which he would soon become familiar:

From the Queen's Head	Yards
To the Dragon	1020
To the World's End	1340
To the Salutation	640
To the Granby	700
To the Chapel	280
To the Old Spaw	640
To the Tewit Well	815
To the Sulphur Wells	1840
To ditto by the footpath	1210
To the Cold Bath	1360
To the Toy-Shop and library	500
To Knaresborough Bridge	4400[5]

When the visitors had accomplished their obligatory spa promenade, they had a leisurely breakfast 'at separate tables', then spent the rest of the day relaxing on excursions by carriage to the surrounding countryside – including visits to picturesque and historic Knaresborough or, if the weather was inclement, staying indoors to read, play cards, billiards and so forth. After dinner they could attend a public ball, usually on Mondays and Fridays. It was mainly then that Blind Jack provided the music for dancing, but it was also part of his job to play during the breakfast times.

It is important to realise that young Metcalf now found himself in prolonged contact with high society in a way that he could never have known as an itinerant musician. An observation made in 1731, just before he started work at the spa, gives us a good idea of the wealthier world into which he entered:

> Of all the watering places I know, Harrogate is, in my opinion, the most charming… with the greatest civility, cheerfulness and good humour, there is a certain rural plainness and freedom mixed, which is very pleasing… Gentlemen of the country, and women of birth and fortune, wives, sisters and daughters, are, for the most part, the company. There were at least four score ladies in the country-dances every night, while I was there, and among them, many fine women.[6]

Though unable to appreciate it fully, Blind Jack must have felt that these balls would be a splendid sight, with the well-to-do guests in their glittering finery, dancing in what was a generously spacious setting for this remote part of Yorkshire. Although referring to a later period, after the Long Room was built, one visitor wrote of his stay at the Queen's Head: 'There is a room that dines with ease one hundred and twenty persons, with fifty servants attending.'[7]

The new young fiddler from Knaresborough was an immediate success, and was set for a steady career as the principal musician:

Metcalf was well received by the nobility and gentry, who employed no other fiddler, except a boy whom he hired as an assistant, when they began to build a long-room at the Queen's Head.[8]

All the known references to Blind Jack confirm that he was exceptionally popular. It was not just a matter of sympathy for a fifteen-year-old boy who was blind. He was growing tall and handsome, carried himself well, had a friendly manner and a mischievous sense of humour. In addition, the way he spoke would appeal to visitors from distant parts of the country. He made no concessions, but expressed himself in the North Riding dialect of Knaresborough, with rich vowels and vocabulary going back to the Angles and Vikings, such as the characteristic vowel in *doon* (down) and *thoo* (thou). We know that he was a habitual dialect speaker, partly from reported snatches of his conversation, and partly because the amanuensis to whom he gave details of his life confessed how he had to struggle to understand 'a language intelligible to those only who are well acquainted with the Yorkshire dialect'.[9]

It was not, however, simply that Blind Jack was seen as a colourful local character. Everything suggests that he was appreciated for the quality of his violin playing, and also for his oboe playing, which he occasionally provided, especially when in a small band or when playing out of doors. His services were in constant demand – and not only at the Queen's Head. Just as the building of the Long Room here – essentially to improve facilities for dancing – had necessitated the appointment of an assistant violinist, so the building of a Long Room at the Green Dragon (first in Hargrove's list) meant a further expansion for Blind Jack.

About this time there was a long-room built at the Green Dragon at Harrogate. More music being then wanted, he engaged one Midgeley (one of the Leeds waits) and his son, as assistants. Midgeley, senior, being a good performer, was taken into partnership gratis; but the son, and Metcalf's former assistant, paid five pounds each premium. This was with the approbation of all the innkeepers, who wished to keep Metcalf at the head of the band.[10]

The fact that Jack was already being invited to play at dances in various prestigious country houses shows that he was considered a first-rate fiddler. Some of these invitations were to the stately homes of well-connected squires, officers and members of the nobility. Amongst the most frequent visitors to the spa was Squire Blackett of Newby Hall near Ripon, who invited Jack to come and play for him at country dances. On one occasion, on returning from Newby Hall, Metcalf, with his assistant (the latter incapable of providing assistance because he was 'much in liquor'), had to swim across the River Ure. In doing so he lost his waistcoat in which were 'the three joints of his hautboy (oboe)' – though he later recovered his silver shoe buckles and 17 shillings, presumably his fee.[11]

One of his most faithful admirers and patrons was Francis Barlow, Squire of Middlethorpe, near York. In the 1735 season, when Barlow had been made High Sheriff of York, he was at Harrogate, and got talking to Metcalf, now a more mature eighteen year old. Finding they had a common interest in hunting, Mr Barlow, who kept a pack of beagles, liked Jack so much that he invited him to spend the winter at Middlethorpe Hall. He duly arrived, riding his own horse, and he was soon going out hunting with Barlow's hounds twice a week.

On the days when he was not hunting it had been arranged that 'Mr Hebdin an eminent musician of York', should come to the hall to practice the violin with him and give him free lessons and advice. This could only have been John Hebden, a player of the cello and

Middlethorpe Hall, near York.

bassoon, active in York from 1733. He was also a composer, notably of 'Six Concertos in Seven Parts' (Opus 2, 1745). Around the time of Jack's stay at Middlethorpe, a benefit concert for Hebden was held in the York Assembly Rooms in 1736, the directors recording that he had 'serv'd the consert in a very oblidgeing and diligent manner'.[12] This alternate pattern of enjoyment outdoors with the hunt and enjoyment indoors with an experienced fellow musician must have constituted one of the happiest periods of Jack's life. And he got on so well with everybody that his stay lasted six months.[13]

A visit to Middlethorpe Hall today (now a fine country hotel and restaurant) gives us an idea of the privileged and comfortable lifestyle that young Metcalf was able to enjoy. Built in 1702 by Thomas Barlow, the Sheffield ironmaster, it had two wings added by his son Francis and retains much of its early eighteenth-century character. This hall has an imposing staircase with ornately carved balustrades. There is a dining room surrounded by beautiful pilasters, and there is the former ballroom, with its tall windows and delicately-plastered ceiling, where we can imagine Blind Jack playing for Francis Barlow's assembled guests.

Set in 20 acres of gardens and parkland, it is no wonder that in 1713 Lady Mary Wortley Montagu, who once lived here with her family, had described Middlethorpe Hall as 'a very pretty place'.[14]

It was at the conclusion of his six months of winter break at Middlethorpe that Blind Jack gave one of his most remarkable performances – though not on any musical instrument. It took place in the hours of darkness at the close of his last day with the Barlows, a spring day at the beginning of the 1736 season when Jack would reach his nineteenth birthday. Having spent the morning on what he called his 'farewell hunt' with the squire and his beagles, he prepared for his journey to Knaresborough by ensuring that both he and his horse had partaken of ample food and drink. First, he rode into York, whose streets by now he had got to know well. His intention was to call and say goodbye to Mr Hebden, his fellow musician, but as he was riding along Coney Street the landlord of the George Inn, by the name of Standish, called out and asked him to stop.

He explained that he had a guest in the inn who required a guide to take him to Harrogate – a distance of some 24 miles. As Standish knew that Jack was going in that direction he thought he might like to earn some money by taking the gentleman with him. Jack agreed, but told the landlord not to say anything to his guest about his being blind. After a farewell drink the two rode off, Jack's horse leading the way.

It was still light as they rode along Ousegate, and someone in the street, recognising Metcalf, shouted out: 'Squire Barlow's blind huntsman!'[15] As the gentleman riding behind Jack was a stranger to the area, this meant nothing to him, especially as Jack, wearing his broad-brimmed hat, was taking care his eyes should not be seen. They rode on through Micklegate, left the city walls behind them at the Bar, and were soon on the rough road in open countryside. Jack had often ridden his horse between York and Knaresborough, and his remarkable memorising of the route now served him well as they rode on through Poppleton Field and Hessay Moor, over Skip Bridge and on towards the grounds of Allerton Mauleverer Castle. Here Jack was anxious not to miss the road which went in a westerly direction towards Knaresborough. Remembering that it started opposite a gate in the high wall surrounding the Allerton estate, he stopped his horse as soon as he felt a blast of wind coming through the gateway on his right. He experienced some difficulty in opening the gate to the Knaresborough road, but the gentleman helped him, still unaware of his guide's handicap.

It was dark by the time they rode through Knaresborough, Jack declining the gentleman's suggestion that they should stop and take a glass of wine at one of the inns, where, of course, he would be well known. As it was, somebody called out: 'That's Blind Jack!', but another voice said this was a mistake, and, once again, the gentleman remained, as Metcalf apparently put it, 'in the dark'.

They rode down High Street, through Bond End and over High Bridge. Instead of being able to take a direct route through Starbeck to Harrogate – the excellent turnpike road that Metcalf would eventually build – they had to follow a rough winding track over Forest Moor and eventually came to High Harrogate, the gentleman unwittingly helping Jack by telling him when he could see a light to their right. For a reason we shall soon refer to, the blind guide took them, not to the Queen's Head, but to the first inn they came to – then known as the Royal Oak, later the Granby.

The hour was so late that the ostler had already gone to bed, so Metcalf, who knew the inn well, led the horses to the stable, while the gentleman settled down over a tankard of hot negus. He then asked his guide to join him for a drink, but noticed that when Jack reached for his tankard a second time his hand went wide of the mark as he groped about

The Royal Oak, High Harrogate.

for it. Assuming that he must have been drinking heavily, he broached the subject with the landlord as soon as Jack left the room, and the following convincingly reported exchange took place:

'I think, landlord,' said the gentleman, 'My guide must have drunk a great deal of spirits since we came here.'
'Why, my good Sir, do you think so?'
'Well, I judge so from the appearance of his eyes.'
'Eyes! Bless you, Sir,' rejoined the landlord, 'Do you not know that he is blind?'
'What do you mean by that?'
'I mean, Sir, that he cannot see.'
'Blind! Gracious God!'
'Yes, Sir. As blind as a stone, by heaven!'
'Well, landlord,' said the gentleman, 'This is too much. Call him in!'
Metcalf enters.
'My friend, are you really blind?'
Yes, Sir. I lost my sight when six years old.'
'Had I known that, I would not have ventured with you for an hundred pounds!'
'And I, Sir,' said Metcalf, 'Would not have lost my way for a thousand.' [16]

The two now spent the remaining hours before bedtime in warm conviviality, drinking plentifully, with Jack playing a new violin that had just arrived for him from London. The anonymous gentleman was so pleased with him that he gave him two guineas that evening, and paid for Jack's food and drink the next day.

This episode is of particular interest. In spite of suggestions that Metcalf, a likeable rogue, was given to fanciful fabrication, the anecdote has the ring of truth. His ability to act as a guide – especially at night-time and in fog, when it is a blind man who has an advantage – is well attested. From his childhood explorations to the very end of his life, Blind Jack – no doubt making the most of his acute hearing, the assistance of his dogs and horses, and his phenomenally accurate memory – was that apparent contradiction in terms, a blind guide.

The principal reason that Jack had guided this gentleman to the Royal Oak rather than the Queen's Head, to which he was returning, was that here the landlord and his wife, the Bensons, had daughters. It was Dorothy Benson, then aged about eighteen, the same age as himself, who interested Jack. We can imagine that he would therefore have lingered at the Royal Oak as long as possible before moving on to the Queen's Head to resume his work for the 1736 summer season.

Here he was welcomed back with enthusiasm, and so much appreciated for his 'jocular and comic' style that he was invited to play at all the other half-dozen Harrogate inns, where he was offered free quarters for himself and his horse. It was at the Green Dragon that Metcalf got to know the two nephews of Mr Boddy, the landlord. These young men, keen to have a day's hunting, asked Jack if he could borrow the Knaresborough pack of hounds kept by Mr Woodburn. So he went to see his old friend the day before the proposed hunt, but his request for the hounds had to be refused. Woodburn was required to have them ready the next morning on Scotton Moor for a man of some importance, Squire Trapps.

As often happened with Blind Jack, he acted on Francis Bacon's principle that 'a wise man makes more opportunities than he finds', and with a wilfulness that bordered on the criminal, got up before dawn the next day and rode off, taking a good hound of his own, to where Woodburn's hounds were kept near High Bridge at Knaresborough. By tweaking the ears of his own hound to make him yell, and at the same time bawling out 'Halloo!', he managed to lure eighteen of the hounds to come out to him. He took them to Harrogate, then a further 5 miles out onto the moors, where the two nephews started hunting hares. But Woodburn had followed him, and the aged Metcalf later recalled how the hound-master's understandable wrath nearly led to his undoing:

> Just at that moment up came Mr Woodburn, foaming with anger, swearing most terribly, and threatening to send Metcalf to the devil, or at least to the house of correction; and, his passion rising to the utmost, rode up with the intention to horse-whip him, which Metcalf prevented, by galloping out of his reach.[17]

Yet, even this, the rogue was able to turn to his advantage. He rode back and apologised, saying he had misunderstood the day the hounds were required. Woodburn's anger eventually cooled, and together they returned with the hounds to where Squire Trapps and his party had been waiting for them for two hours. Metcalf joined in his second hunt, then at three in the afternoon returned to his friends at the Green Dragon, where that evening they dined well on a brace of newly caught hares, and where he recalled 'after spending many jovial hours, he played country dances till daylight.'[18]

There can be no doubt that Blind Jack knew how to enjoy himself, and that he was well known in all the Harrogate inns as a young bon vivant, the life and soul of many a late-night party, where they plied him with drink in return for his playing. He seemed to be able to turn his hand to whatever he fancied, never allowing his blindness to restrict his full enjoyment of life. He even learnt to play bowls, to the delight of spa visitors. They would watch him start a match on the basis of his being allowed an extra bowl 'for the deficiency of an eye', as he put it, so that he had three bowls instead of one. It was noticed that he had a friend standing near the jack, and another midway, his flow of conversation with them helping him to judge the distances. He was especially famous for his card playing, and his uncanny skill in knowing what the cards were by their feel. 'Many were the persons of rank who, from curiosity, played with him,' he recalled, adding that he generally won the majority of the card games.[19]

Nothing is more obvious than that Metcalf played games essentially to make money. From his cockfighting days onwards, he was an inveterate gambler. Between his engagements as a fiddler he found plenty of time to take his horse to local races, entering it for plates and prizes, and placing bets. Racing was held on the level green of the Stray, adjacent to the Queen's Head, and an actual racecourse was laid out here, but not until 1793.[20] So it became the custom for Blind Jack to visit established racecourses within reach of a horse-ride, particularly the one at York. Here he mingled with the crowds, and from them and the jockeys received helpful tips about the horses.[21]

In High Harrogate, where he bred his own horses, like his father before him, young Metcalf was known as a kind of 'horse whisperer'. For example, he trained his horses to respond by neighing when he called out their names, and was said to be able by this means to select his own animals from any number in a field.[22] He had such an affinity with horses that, when it came to his frequent transactions as a horse-dealer he was, as William Grainge later put it, 'an excellent judge of horse-flesh'. As evidence of this he noted the tradition of how Jack could always pick out a horse with defective sight:

> He coaxed the animal until he had made acquaintance with it, then, placing one hand over its heart, passed the other smartly before its eyes, without touching them. If it could see, a sudden heart-throb told Jack the fact… If not, he concluded that, like himself, the horse was deprived of sight.[23]

He made use of his own horses for wagers, even riding them himself round a mile-long circular course, marked out by posts. On one occasion he offered to ride three circuits of this course, competing against other riders. A blind rider was at such an obvious disadvantage that only those with experience of Jack's flair for ingenuity would have considered him a safe bet. How on earth could he even contemplate taking part in such a race? A pity we do not have his original account in early dialect, but this is how his clever strategy was written up:

> He procured four dinner bells from different inns – and placing a man with a bell at each post, he was enabled, by the ringing, to turn; and fully availing himself of the superior fleetness of his horse, came in winner, amidst the plaudits and exultations of the multitude, except only those who betted against him.[24]

On another occasion he galloped his horse in a wager with a man called Skelton, riding over boggy ground near the Old Spa. This time he arranged for a friend to stand beyond the point where the terms of the bet required him to stop. There he arranged for his friend to sing a song – and to keep on singing, so he could be guided by the sound. Once again he won his wager.[25]

By the age of twenty-one, then, Blind Jack had built himself a reputation, not merely as a spa musician and horseman, but as a notorious drinker and versatile gambler. It is not surprising that he was also known as a womaniser – an intriguing aspect of his life that deserves a chapter to itself.

Chapter Four

Amours and Adventures

Blind Jack's determination to lead a normal life meant that he sought the company of young women. Or rather it was they who sought his company, because there is every indication that they found him attractive, both in his strong physique and his lively, outgoing personality.

One of the first girls to take the initiative was Dolly Benson, daughter of the landlord of the Royal Oak previously referred to. The way she set her cap at Jack, fussing over him and doing him special favours, was first noticed during the horse races that he organised on the Stray close to the inns. Dolly, with her friends, always made a point of attending a race, and used to offer to supply him with extra corn for his horses, which she could get from her father's store. Back inside the Royal Oak:

> Metcalf began to wonder much at it; she acted as chamber-maid, and would frequently ask him to sit down, and would sit down by him, and would have a little negus or some other liquor. The lady and Metcalf became very intimate, and this intimacy produced mutual regard and confidence.[1]

Dolly's mother, however, even more than her father, did not approve of this friendship. She made it clear that she intended her daughter to marry into a higher social rank than the one to which Metcalf belonged. There is no mention of objections because of his blindness, though this would have seemed an obvious burden for their daughter to have to share. The essential objection was apparently the fact that he came from a working-class family, and had no conceivable career prospects.

In order to conceal from Dolly's parents their growing attraction for each other, the two devised a code which allowed them to talk together, making arrangements to meet, for example, without their parents suspecting anything. Their system was for Jack to refer to himself as 'Mary' or 'Tibby' and for Dolly to call herself 'Harry', 'Dicky' or some other boy's name. Jack might say to her: 'You must tell Richard that Mary will be here' – on a particular day. If Dolly's mother overheard, and asked who this was, she would reply that it concerned a girl her brother was going to meet.

Jack, however, perhaps when he was playing the fiddle here, contrived to have the occasional use of a bedroom at the Royal Oak, in a different part of the inn from where Dolly slept. On one occasion they had arranged a secret assignation, and at midnight he climbed in through an open window, and was going up the stairs to find Dolly's room, when he bumped into her mother. She angrily asked what he was doing there at this hour, to which he replied that he had come in late and fallen asleep by the fire. Mrs Benson apparently accepted the explanation, and told Dolly to take him to the room set aside for him.[2]

This anecdote strongly suggests that the couple had a physical relationship. The writer says that their intimacy resulted from 'frequent intercourse' – and although this eighteenth-century usage does not in any way imply sexual intercourse, this may well have been the case. Evidence that Jack did a certain amount of sleeping around is found in the account of an affair with another woman – which must have been at the same time he was having this clandestine relationship with Dolly.

The incident took place when Jack was back in Knaresborough, living at his old home near the church. This was during the winter season, when there was no work for him at the spa. In the town were two young men of his acquaintance, whose sister lived with them, working as their housekeeper. When Jack called to see them, she used to joke with him so freely that he did not take her seriously when one day she said she would come to his bedroom very late at night, and that he must leave the door of the house unlocked. It is not clear whether Metcalf had the place to himself, but he refers to it as 'his mother's house' at this point.

Deciding that this young woman might, after all, have been serious, Jack left the door unlocked, and waited. 'At the dead-time of night', we read, she duly came to the cottage, 'unawed at passing by the church, whose sanction was wanting'. This is all that the editor tells us about what was obviously a sexual encounter, except that his moralistic reticence allows him to add, 'Metcalf, too, had unfortunately left his scruples at another house'.

A few months later this woman, no longer jocular, greeted him with the melodramatic and predictable words:

'I am ruined! Undone! Lost for ever, if you do not make an honest woman of me!'
'What's the matter?' quoth Jack
'Enough!' says she. 'I am with child.'[3]

She was so sure that Jack would marry her that she sent a quantity of linen for him to keep, ready for when she would move in. But, in spite of having been disloyal to Dolly, he knew her to be his true love, and that she was the only one he had any intention of marrying.

For a while he busied himself with other matters, such as his passion for horse dealing. There is a particularly convincing account, replete with prices and technical equestrian details, of how he made a good profit through his clever negotiation and expert knowledge of horses. One day he met a huntsman who had a horse to sell, for which he was asking twenty-five guineas. Jack trotted it for a mile or two, then returned it to the stable, saying that there was something wrong with its eyes, and that it would soon be blind. The huntsman refused to lower his price, saying that his horse was 'beautifully moulded, only six years old, and his action good'.

Jack then took the owner into the stable and asked him to lay his hands upon the horse's eyes, as he had done. Did he not feel 'their uncommon heat' – a sign of serious inflammation? How could he, in all conscience, ask such a high price for a horse that was going blind? After more bargaining Jack purchased the horse, bridle and saddle, not for twenty-five guineas, but £14.

The story of the horse does not end here. Jack's diagnosis of incipient blindness proved correct. As he was riding on his new purchase on common land near the Harrogate Toy Shop, the horse ran into a signpost, and nearly threw him.[4] Even so, he set off to ride to Ripon, where he was to play that night at an assembly. As he passed the World's End inn he overtook another rider going to Ripon, and wagered with him 'six penny-worth of liquor' that he would reach the next alehouse before him. On the way his horse stumbled on the rough road, throwing him to the ground and falling across him. As he struggled to get up, one of its fore-shoes cut into Metcalf's face. He remembered that a passing minister, 'the Revd Mr Richardson', had come up to see if he was all right, and that he had told him that his only complaint was the cowardice of the horse, 'who had struck him while he was down'.

As the fall had damaged his violin, when he got to Ripon he had to borrow one, and was now coming to the conclusion that he would have to sell this newly-purchased animal. Fine though it was in other respects, its inflamed eyes were now seriously discharging pus. However, he applied 'the usual remedies of alum blown into the eyes, rowelling in different parts etc.', found this made a big improvement, and took the horse, now 'in marketable condition', to the big horse show outside Micklegate Bar in York. A well-known dealer called Carter showed an interest in it. So Jack offered to trot in for a while, saying that with his own great weight (he was said to weigh seventeen stone) any fault in the animal would immediately be seen. The price was twenty-two guineas. Carter offered him sixteen, then seventeen – which he gladly accepted.

He now had to walk all the way back to Harrogate, but on the way made yet another wager, 'for two shillings worth of punch', with a Knaresborough man who let him take it in turns to ride his horse, each riding for a mile while the other walked. Jack mounted the horse for his first turn, suggesting to his companion that he would ride on to a little way beyond Poppleton Field, and when he saw a certain gate there on the right he would tether the horse to it, and proceed to walk the next mile. The horse's owner agreed, but found no horse at the gate, and was obliged to walk the whole way to Knaresborough. At first enraged, he finally laughed when Blind Jack made his plea that he simply had not seen the gate.[5]

An incident which must have taken his mind off his love affairs was his pub fight with a notorious Knaresborough heavyweight called John Bake, who was:

> …a man of ferocious temper and athletic figure. He was considered in the neighbourhood as a champion, or rather bully; and thus qualified, was often employed specially to serve writs or warrants, in cases where desperate resistance was expected.[6]

At the time John Metcalf was twenty-one, and in spite of his major handicap, a fair match for Bake. Blind Jack was 'six feet one inch and a half tall, broad in proportion and remarkably robust withal'. We are not told in which of Knaresborough's many alehouses the encounter took place. It could have been the Hart's Horn in Silver Street, dating from 1712, or the Crown in High Street, dating from 1731, or one of several no longer extant, but it is interestingly described as a 'public house', one of the very early uses of this term. Jack had gone there with a friend, who sat down with Bake to play a game of cards.

During the game Bake took some money off the table. When Jack's friend objected that he was not entitled to this, Bake jumped up and struck him a violent blow. Jack shouted out in defence of his friend, so Blake punched him as well. Jack lunged towards his unseen opponent, managed to grapple with him, and started to give him such a terrible beating that Bake cried out for mercy. He was so impressed by Jack's enormous strength and skill as a boxer that he later offered to bet on him as a prize-fighter.[7]

After yet more wagers – including a race from Harrogate to Knaresborough Market Cross, which Metcalf won by swimming across the Nidd – there was a hunt, at the conclusion of which he was suddenly brought back to the reality of the serious consequences of having made this woman pregnant. His invitation to join the fox hunt in Belmont Wood, near Knaresborough, came from gentlemen at the Queen's Head who had been impressed on seeing how he handled another horse Metcalf had just bought very cheaply. As Jack told them, this horse could jump 'over any well or fence, the height of himself'.

The hunt moved from Belmont Wood towards Plumpton Rocks, the hounds in pursuit of a fine fox. He led them for about 6 miles, finally returning to cross the River Nidd near the site of Knaresborough Priory. Jack, having lost his hat in the strong wind, decided he would ride across the river at Chaffy Dam (as it is now known). He had often crossed here on foot, and thought that by using the sound of the long waterfall of the weir as a guide, he could steer his horse across. But it stumbled on the slippery stones, and was sent floundering into the river:

> …away went horse and rider into the dam. Metcalf had the presence of mind to disengage his feet from the stirrups… but both the horse and himself were immersed over head in water.[8]

He managed to get to the opposite bank, empty the water from his boots, remount his nag and follow the hounds to the north-east of Knaresborough, where the fox went to earth at the Coney-Garths. The hunting party, accepting defeat, went with Jack on to the inn at Scriven, and it was here, while he was drying out, and joining the others in a drink, that he heard from the landlord a piece of unwelcome news.

He was told that the woman who was requiring him to marry her had 'gone that day to filiate a child to him' – that is, to declare in law that the child to whom she had now given birth had been fathered by John Metcalf, who would be held responsible, and expected to marry the woman or provide compensation. The landlord warned him that a warrant had been issued, and that it would be served upon him if he rode through Knaresborough.[9]

Old print of Jack's fall into the Nidd.

Jack made light of his predicament, telling his friends, with his customary fondness for wordplay, that it could not be true that he was the father, because he could assure them that 'he had not seen the woman for several years'. Underneath his levity he was, however, very worried about what this would do to his relationship with Dolly. He managed to get safely back to Harrogate, where he took his assistant fiddler into his confidence, wisely telling him: 'Ah mun speak wi' Dorothy Benson, for she will certainly hear of this, and I had better be the first messenger.' A meeting was arranged in one of the inns, and he told her what had happened. Her response was generous, forgiving and practical:

> 'Ah John!' replied she. 'Thou hast got into a bad scrape, but I intreat thee, do not think of marrying her'. He told her solemnly he would not.[10]

He now decided that, with his assistant, he should go to Knaresborough to try to find out what the situation was. They were half way there when his companion whispered to Jack that the town officer was coming towards them. He was Jonathan Knowles, a Quaker, part of the small but active Knaresborough group of members of the Society of Friends, who had built a meeting house in Gracious Street in 1701.[11] As town officer he would be one of two unpaid constables appointed annually to keep the peace, and who had the authority to serve warrants. Being a Quaker, Knowles made habitual use of 'thou/thee', normal in local dialect (as used by Jack and Dolly) but noted in what Jack remembered of his more standard speech:

> 'Stop, I want to speak to thee!' He then explained his errand, and pressed Metcalf much to marry the woman, to whom he replied that he had no thoughts of marriage, as he did not understand housekeeping, and was so young – and desired to know whether for thirty or forty pounds the matter might be made up (but at the time Metcalf did not know how he could acquire five pounds). 'Yea, friend', said Jonathan, 'Perhaps I can settle the affair for thee on those terms.'[12]

Jack then proposed that they should return to Harrogate, accompanied by the officer. There he promised he would find the money and hand it over. The Quaker accepted, and they all went to the Royal Oak, where Jack drank a tankard of punch with the officer, then said it would take him at least an hour to collect this money from various sources in Harrogate – so the officer must wait there, drink up his punch, 'and call for more'. Jonathan Knowles, with Jack's assistant to keep him company, was naive enough to agree to this, and settled down to his drinking.

Jack did not return to the Royal Oak, but hid in a nearby wood till the coast was clear. What he later heard was that the Quaker had gone round the spa asking people: 'Friend. Has thou perchance seen a blind fiddler?' One gentleman, aware of the Quaker disapproval of music and dancing, apparently remarked that he was surprised that a person dressed as a Quaker should want a fiddler. 'I tell thee,' replied the town officer, 'I want one at this time'. But after fruitless enquiries he went back to Knaresborough.

Realising that if he continued to work in public as a fiddler, he could be arrested at any time, Jack decided to run for cover and lie low in a place he had heard so much about from spa visitors – the great metropolis of London. He would not attempt to go south by a direct route, but by a circuitous and much easier way. Having arranged with his assistant and a nearby relation to look after his affairs, he saddled his horse and set off to the coast, making for Scarborough.

Taking the waters, Low
Harrogate.

A horseback journey of nearly 60 miles might well have seemed utterly impossible for a blind rider with no one to guide him. But on this, as on many other such journeys, Blind Jack relied on one infallible guide – the horse itself. Provided it could see the way ahead, with hedges, walls or fences on each side, a good horse could make its way with little direction from the rider. A contemporary instance of this is found in the journal of John Wesley, the horseback evangelist, who rode some 250,000 miles, much of it while 'giving the horse its head' so he could get on with his reading. 'I throw the reins on its neck,' he wrote, following the practice, as Metcalf did, of 'riding with a slack rein'.[13]

Scarborough, 'the Queen of the Watering Places', had been a rival to 'Knaresborough Spa' in the previous century, as evidenced by the amusingly vitriolic exchanges between Dr Robert Wittie, who praised the waters of Scarborough, and Dr George Tonstall, who poured scorn on them, claiming that they produced jaundice, and had a similar petrifying effect to those of the Dropping Well. He had worked in Scarborough, but now championed the waters of 'the Knaresborough Spaw', in particular those of the Tewit Well.[14] Jack perhaps had at the back of his mind the possibility of earning money at Scarborough Spa as a fiddler, but this would have meant that this new whereabouts could easily have been reported by the gossipy health seekers who went round from spa to spa, including the common move between Scarborough and Harrogate.

He must have taken an interest in what he refers to as 'the Spa', with its saline and chalybeate springs – one still to be seen – on the very edge of the shore. But all he related of his brief stay there is a memory of how he was nearly carried out to sea. Walking on the sands near the spa one day, he was tempted to have a swim, the boundless ocean offering an exciting prospect to one who had so far only been able to swim in the narrow reaches of the Yorkshire rivers. He asked a friend to look after his clothes, and to give him a shout when he saw that he had swum out far enough from the shore. The friend duly shouted as loud as he could, but could not make Jack hear above the noise of the waves, and was dismayed to see him carried out of sight. Jack, however, realising the danger, turned over on his back and floated, listening intently. He then found he could hear the breakers beating against the end of the stone pier, and was able to use the sound to guide him as he swam back to safety.[15]

This flourishing seaside spa was now introducing sea bathing and bathing machines as part of its treatment, and Jack must have found it made an interesting comparison with Harrogate. He did not stay long, however, but rode sixteen or so miles north to the small sea port of Whitby, where an aunt of his lived. He says that her house was 'near the alum works', which probably means that it would be just to the north of Whitby at Sandsend, because the other sites where the alum shale was processed were too far north, or – in the case of the well-known works at Robin Hood's Bay – too far south, to be described as 'at Whitby'. The alum industry, dating from around 1600, was then prospering on this part of the Yorkshire coast, the local alum-bearing shale being piled up in great heaps with brushwood and gorse, and kept burning for as long as a year. The final product of white crystals was exported from Yorkshire, valued for its use in tanning, dyeing and medicine.[16]

Jack stayed with his aunt until he could manage to get himself a passage on a ship bound for London. Leaving his horse with his aunt, he went into Whitby and boarded this vessel with its cargo of alum, no doubt helping to work his passage by playing his fiddle and telling his stories. In London, with his usual enterprise, he made useful contacts, and was soon being invited to play at dances, where 'he played on the violin, and did very well'. These contacts, however, seem to have been with people he had got to know at Harrogate, and whose links with the spa made him feel that, even in London, he was not out of the reach of the long arm of the law. So, hearing of another ship that was about to set sail for Whitby, he left London after only a few weeks, and returned to his aunt's.

As restless as ever, within a short while he was off again, this time taking a ship from Whitby, sailing 60 miles or so north to Newcastle, in the mid-1700s a prospering city and the chief port of Tyneside. He had made the acquaintance of several well-placed families there, who had visited Harrogate before the affair of his being affiliated, and who would have no prejudice against him. On the contrary, he was heartily welcomed as a fiddler at many family gatherings, and was handsomely treated by Councillor Grey, 'an eminent man of the law', who invited Metcalf to dine with him every day throughout the period he stayed in Newcastle, which was about a month. This must have been George Grey (1713-1746) of Southwick Hall, north of Sunderland, whose daughter, Elizabeth, later married Charles, first Earl Grey (a different family, later associated with 'Earl Grey's tea'). George Grey was indeed eminent in legal advice and transactions in Newcastle, as well as being noted for his hospitality as a country gentleman.[17]

Councillor Grey must have been as tall and well built as Jack, because one day he offered him one of his suits, perhaps having noticed how shabby his clothes were. Jack was delighted to have, not some old cast-off, but the finest outfit he had ever worn:

> …waistcoat, breeches, shoes and stockings: everything fitted as though they had been made for him. The clothes were silk grogram and very little worse for wear, a very handsome dress.[18]

Soon afterwards he moved on, this time down to Sunderland, where – no doubt seeking another ship – he 'stayed a little while among the sailors', presumably not showing off his gentleman's attire. Then he was back in Whitby, staying with his aunt, and reunited with his horse.

Impatient to be with Dolly again, and also anxious to find out if he was still being sought by the authorities, Blind Jack decided he would risk going back to Knaresborough and Harrogate. He had made good friends in Whitby – as he always did, wherever he stayed – and so his aunt gathered them together for a farewell party. 'They had plenty of flip and bumbo and other sorts of liquor, and got pretty merry'.[19] Jack was so generous in paying for drinks, that he ended up with only a guinea to take with him – and this he lost on the first day of his journey. He rode through Pickering and Malton, then on towards York. As he approached Crome Beck his horse began to tire, and he was obliged to wade across, leading the horse through the swollen water and through muddy ground near Lobster House – still to be seen as Lobster Cottage, and with a tradition that Blind Jack stayed there.[20]

He managed to find the way across Stockton Moor by taking his direction from the crowing of a cock, then followed a paved causeway into the city of York. Here he remembers riding through the streets he was already familiar with – Goodramgate, the Shambles, the Pavement, and over Ouse Bridge – eventually getting out of the city to reach Middlethorpe Hall by dawn. Having been so well received here before, he could count on further hospitality. But he found the gates locked, and had to climb over their spiked tops, hoisting himself up by means of the rein and bridle removed from his horse. Once inside, he opened the gates and led in his horse – to the astonishment of some women servants who were up early doing the washing.

As expected, he was welcomed by the Barlow family, glad to have him for a while as their favourite fiddler. He stayed with them for about three weeks, using his time to make discreet enquiries amongst the servants about whether or not it was safe for him to go back to Knaresborough. The news was good. He was assured that the woman whose baby he had fathered was 'troublesome to nobody, but maintained herself and child, so no person had any reason to make a disturbance'.[21]

So he set off for Knaresborough and Harrogate, full of confidence, longing to be in the arms of his beloved Dolly once again, and ready to settle down and become her lawfully wedded husband. But his vagabond existence as an itinerant fiddler was not yet over – and he was soon to be confronted by the biggest challenge of his whole life.

Commemorative mug sold in Blind Jack's lifetime.

Chapter Five

Travels and Troubles: Love finds a Way

Young John Metcalf was in high spirits when he arrived in Knaresborough on his way to resume his work at the spa. Although it was not until late evening when he rode into town, he had soon gathered together his friends and fellow musicians. They were delighted at his return, and wanted to celebrate, not only by drinking, but by making music in the streets.

With Jack leading lively music on his oboe, off they went:

> ...they had a new country dance, which was called Tit for Tat. They played that tune through all the streets of Knaresbro' that night, and many people wondered what was the meaning of it, which was to show that Metcalf had arrived, and that he did not come in secret, but in a lively manner.[1]

The song referred to could only have been the newly written bawdy piece 'A Frolicsome Sea Captain' – or 'Tit for Tat'. It tells how a wealthy captain seduces the wife of one of his sailors, paying her fifty guineas for a night:

> All you that delight in a frolicsome song,
> I'll tell you a story before it be long;
> It's of a sea captain, a frolicsome spark,
> Who played with a sailor's fair wife in the dark

The sailor, hidden under the bed, steals the adulterer's fine uniform, dresses up in it, and manages to get into the captain's house and sleep with his wife:

> So he tit for tat with the captain did play
> And slept in her arms till the break of the day.[2]

We are not told whether Blind Jack and his musicians sang any of the well-written verses (twenty-six in all!), but they would have made the most of the jolly tune. (See Appendix A.)

The next day Jack went on to Harrogate, making a similarly bold arrival, this time by wearing the suit given to him by Councillor Grey, and making 'a grander appearance than they had ever seen him before'. He received a very warm reception after his long absence, including a happy reunion with Dolly – though they still felt it wise to meet in secret.

For a while Jack settled down to his usual employment of playing at the Queen's Head during breakfast and at the evening dances. As before, he managed to fit in sessions at other inns and at grand houses where gentlemen provided entertainment for their guests. On his rounds he met other musicians, and in particular renewed a friendship with a man he had met in Newcastle who played the 'small pipes' – another name for the Northumbrian pipes, which are indeed smaller and different in tone from the better-known Scottish version. This piper had often been to London, where good money could be earned by itinerant musicians. He was soon to make another visit and invited Jack to come with him.

The urge to travel again was still strong, and Jack had enjoyed his earlier brief stay in London sufficiently to want to return. Moreover, there would be the chance to earn far more money than at the spa, where the summer season was now coming to an end, and this would help to make his projected marriage to Dolly a reality.

So he accepted his friend's invitation and the two minstrels set off south, travelling by stagecoach — or so we must assume, as there is no reference to walking or horses. This second visit to London has either been confused or conflated by two fictionalising writers, one following the other, who have incorrectly assumed it to be the visit he made by ship from Whitby.[3] This journey was a new experience for him — and one that would spark off ideas about one day doing something to improve the notoriously bad roads of eighteenth-century England. There were two routes from Harrogate to London. The first was via Harewood, Leeds, Wakefield, Sheffield, Nottingham and Bedford, a distance of 210 miles. The second — which was the one they seem to have taken — was via Wetherby, down the Great North Road to Ferrybridge, Doncaster and beyond, a distance of 199 miles. Both journeys were advertised as taking four days — though whichever route they chose, it would have been perhaps as long as a week. There is no end of evidence about the state of the roads at this time — uneven, full of jagged stones, deep ruts and hollows, with the coach wheels constantly damaged by obstruction, or slowed and brought to a standstill by sinking into boggy ground. Even the stretches of road which the turnpike trusts had recently attempted to drain and level were not much better, as Smollett had noted in his coach journey to Harrogate up the Great North Road:

> Considering the tax we pay for turnpikes, the roads of this county constitute a most intolerable grievance. Between Newark and Wetherby I have suffered more from jolting and swinging than ever I felt in the whole course of my life.[4]

Daniel Defoe, during his extensive travels throughout Britain, had written of similar problems, and Arthur Young, the well-known connoisseur of roads in the eighteenth century, though full of praise for the roads in France, found that many of those in England, especially in the north, shook his coach so badly that they were likely to 'dislocate his bones', and categorised nearly half the roads as 'middling', indifferent', 'bad' and 'vile'.[5] John Metcalf, used to the comparatively steady motion of a horse, which could pick and steer its way, would have found this long and uncomfortable coach ride to London an experience that would not only make him fully aware of the gross deficiencies of our roads, but one so unpleasant that, as we shall see, he must have vowed that he would certainly not use a coach for the return journey.

Although literally seeing the sights of London was denied him, we can assume that Blind Jack, with the help of the piper, took in the atmosphere of the spacious squares and fine buildings, including Westminster Abbey and St Paul's Cathedral, where he would be able to run his fingers over sculptures and inscriptions — and where he would be able to hear choral and orchestral music. In London's parks and gardens, such as Vauxhall, he would have been able to hear, for example, the music of Handel, including 'Water Music', composed in 1715, originally played for George I on barges sailing up the Thames, with its grandiose open-air orchestral sound, and the brilliance of trumpets and drums, something he is unlikely ever to have heard in Yorkshire. It is also possible that at Covent Garden he heard 'The Beggar's Opera', at least one song from which he is known to have included in his repertoire.

Dancing at Harrogate Spa.

His own music making in London may have involved some busking, in company with the piper, but he seems to have used his spa contacts again, and got himself invited to play at dances in the homes of wealthy and aristocratic families, and also profited from his friendship with his fellow musicians, who 'frequented the houses of many gentlemen in town.'[6]

As soon as the winter season was over he had thoughts of returning to Harrogate, but the feeling of spring in the air sent coursing through his veins an urge to experience the countryside to the west of London. He set off on a walking tour through the then comparatively rural Kensington and Hammersmith – and even on to Colnbrook, Maidenhead and Reading. He returned via Windsor and Hampton Court, arriving back in London at the beginning of May 1739.

Waiting for him at his lodgings was a message from a gentleman whom Jack had got to know both at Harrogate and Newcastle. He was Colonel George Liddell, Member of Parliament for Berwick-on-Tweed. Liddell was a very successful Tyneside coal magnate who served Berwick as MP from 1727 to 1734 and again from 1737 to 1740, the year of his death – not long after his meeting with Blind Jack early in 1738.[7] Jack had made use of the open invitation to visit him at his house in King Street, Covent Garden, and now the colonel was about to set off to return to his northern home, Ravensworth Castle near Newcastle. As usual he would be calling at Harrogate for his annual three weeks at the Spa. Would Metcalf like a lift on the outside, 'either behind his coach, or on the top'?[8]

Jack thanked him, but respectfully declined the offer, giving as his reason that he could walk in a day as far as he wished to travel – implying that, from his experience of the roads on his way down, he could get back to Harrogate faster on foot. There is no evidence that

Liddell offered Metcalf 'ten guineas' if by some chance he reached Harrogate before him – a piece of embroidery in the fictional versions of the story. We can be sure, though, that Jack saw this as a kind of wager, something on which he would bet his prowess as a long-distance walker.

Whether or not the two talked in terms of a wager, they both set off at about the same time on that Monday in early May. First, Colonel Liddell, leaving at noon, in his fine coach, accompanied by a suite of 'sixteen servants on horseback'. Then Blind Jack, on foot, setting off an hour earlier, feeling his way, not with a conventional walking stick, but with a longer and thinner one, designed for sweeping and probing, similar to the one seen in the later Metcalf portrait, which shows the actual stick we still possess.

The route taken by both contenders was through Barnet to reach the first agreed stopping-place at Welwyn, north of London.[9] Jack claims that he reached the inn on that first day 'a little before the colonel, who was surprised at his performance'. Having dined at Liddell's expense, Jack was ready to set off early the next day, striding out on the Great North Road, carefully avoiding the boggy ground that would prove such a hindrance to the colonel's coach and party of horsemen.

He soon reached Biggleswade, but there found the flooding of the road so bad that he tried to find a way round by taking a footpath. A stranger noticed that he was wandering about, and came up to offer help, first commenting, Jack recalls, that he looked as though he had been drinking liquor that morning – another confirmation of the scarred cornea also misinterpreted by the man he had guided from York.[10] The stranger led the way along the path and across planks over a sluice, eventually reaching the turnpike, where Jack had to climb over a locked gate.

He was so pleased with the helpfulness of this stranger that he offered him a coin:

'Here, good fellow. Take that, and get thee a pint of beer.' But the other declined it, saying he was welcome. Metcalf, however, pressing the reward upon him, was asked: 'Can you see very well?'
'Not remarkably well,' he replied.
'My friend,' said the stranger, 'I do not mean to tithe you – I am the Rector of this parish. And so, God bless you, and I wish you a good journey.' [11]

Blind Jack pressed on, making for the village of Buckden, south of Huntingdon, where he stayed once again at the inn the colonel had chosen. This was the arrangement at the end of each day – and though he does not claim always to have reached the inn before the colonel, he was certainly able to keep up with him, the coach and equipage forever being slowed down by the state of the roads. It is, incidentally, interesting to see that in Hargrove's first edition of his *History* (1775), he lists staging posts from London to Harrogate almost identical to that mentioned by Metcalf.[12]

By the Saturday, the sixth day after leaving London, both Jack and Colonel Liddell had reached Wetherby, less than 8 miles from Harrogate. As by this time they were exhausted, the colonel proposed that they should all spend the weekend in Wetherby before moving on to Harrogate. Jack excused himself on the grounds that he had urgent matters to attend to, and set off that same night to walk to the spa. He was spurred on by the thought of being with Dolly again – and also, no doubt, by the fact that he would now be able to claim he had reached Harrogate before Colonel Liddell, whom he duly met there on the Monday for a joint celebration.

This account of a man walking from London to Harrogate faster than a coach could travel obviously raises the question of whether John Metcalf was a teller of tall stories like Baron von Munchausen, whose adventures had been translated into English about ten years before Metcalf was writing his memoirs. It is arguable that the eighteenth-century fashion for presenting fantasy in the guise of fact coloured so much of the tales he told to spa visitors. Can his claim to have outmatched Colonel Liddell be taken seriously?

I think it can, for the following reasons. In the first place, Blind Jack had the physique, the long legs and experience – to say nothing of a firm resolution – which equipped him to be an outstanding long-distance walker. To reach Wetherby in five and a half days would have meant an average of rather more than 20 miles a day. This would certainly have been possible. Foster Powell of Horsforth, a contemporary of Metcalf, is said to have taken only five and a half days in 1773 to walk from London to York – and back![13] It is, of course, possible that the resourceful Blind Jack managed to get a lift or two – as he did on other occasions – and that he did not disclose this. But his claim to have walked such distances is certainly credible when we remember it comes from a time when such feats were common – William Wordsworth, for example, tramping many miles a day in the Lake District.

Secondly, the condition of the roads really was bad enough to have slowed down and even halted a coach, so that Metcalf on foot was not really competing with Liddell on a smooth-running and uninterrupted coach ride. The situation is amusingly summed up in the anecdote related by Samuel Smiles of a man with a wooden leg who was offered a lift by a stagecoach. He declined, saying: 'Thank 'ee, but I cannot wait. I am in a hurry.' Then he stumped on, ahead of the stagecoach.[14]

Thirdly, Metcalf would have told his story on many occasions when its veracity could easily have been challenged. Though it did not appear in print until 1795, there would still have been old people in Harrogate who could remember Blind Jack's famous victory over Colonel Liddell. The evidence does not, of course, amount to anything conclusive, but it seems very likely that he did indeed walk all the way from London to Harrogate in a space of time that would have been remarkable even for a sighted man.

The significance of this expedition to London cannot be overestimated. John Metcalf had gained a first-hand knowledge of the appalling state of Britain's roads – both through the coach journey down and his foot slogging back to Harrogate. He had discovered that even the Great North Road was by no means an ideal means of communication, and that Britain's highways in general were a national disgrace. This double journey of over 400 miles must have been a formative experience for him. It would have strengthened his conviction – already gained as a traveller on horseback – that one of these days – if ever he had the opportunity – he would do something about it.

After being separated for seven months, we can imagine that Jack and Dolly would have had a rapturous reunion. They were so much in love that nothing, it seemed, was going to prevent their being married. Indeed, Jack was so sure of her affection that he was not alarmed when he found that in his absence another young man had been showing an interest in Dolly. This suitor, at this point unnamed, even approached Jack and asked him – since he knew Dolly's family so well – if he would put in a good word on his behalf to the Bensons. Reflecting the humour with which the aged Metcalf must later have recalled this, the amanuensis writes: 'This, when made known to the lady by the man of her heart, afforded them both great entertainment.'[15]

For a while the twenty-two-year-old blind aspirant to Dolly's hand in marriage seems to have worked hard to raise money for his intended matrimony. In addition to playing in Harrogate he now made regular journeys with his assistant to Ripon, where he was a popular violinist at this ancient little city's assembly. He lists with pride the patrons of this fashionable gathering: Sir Walter Blacket of Newby Hall (where Eugene Aram, Knaresborough's notorious scholarly murderer, had lived, his father being head gardener there), Sir John Wray, Sir Robert Graham, Squire Rhodes, Squire Aislaby of Studley 'and many others'.[16] Soon he had, by dint of all the extra work, accumulated £15, which for him, and for that period, was a considerable sum. Moreover, he made the sensible decision to hand it over to Dolly, so she could act as his treasurer – knowing very well his besetting vice of frittering away his money on gambling.

It was unfortunate that Dolly was not stricter with him. Before long he persuaded her – presumably on the pretext that he could make more money for them both – to release cash bit by bit, until he eventually lost a total of £10 on his old passion for cockfighting. The rest of his savings went on horseracing at York, and Dolly's loyalty to him was now coming under an understandable strain. What made matters worse was that his addiction to gambling now led to an increase in his drinking:

> ...like all persons who lose money by gaming, he still wanted to get it the same way it went, and he took to drink more than formerly, for sorrow is often dry.[17]

During the summer season of 1738 it looks as though Dolly, remembering 'his former misconduct' with the woman who now had his child, and dismayed by his incorrigible gambling and drinking, was sufficiently disillusioned with her dissolute lover to at least consider the possibility of marriage to somebody else. The young man previously referred to, whom they had both laughingly dismissed, now paid his addresses to her with more ardour, and made a good impression on her mother. He was Anthony Dickinson, a shoemaker in Kirkby Overblow, a village about 4 miles south of Harrogate. The fact that he had sufficient wealth and standing to satisfy the requirement of the Bensons is indicated by the statement that he was not just an ordinary cordwainer working on his own, but employed a number of others.[18] They must have considered this well-heeled shoemaker an ideal match for their daughter.

When he heard that the banns of marriage had been published in the parish churches of Knaresborough and Kirkby Overblow, Jack was utterly dismayed. His astonishment and remorse, as well as his controlled and dignified response to Dolly, is concisely described by the amanuensis:

> Metcalf was much surprised, having long thought himself secure of her affection. He now began to believe that she had laid more stress on his late follies than he had been aware of, and the remembrance of them gave him exquisite pain, for he loved her tenderly, and was restrained from proposing marriage to her only by the doubts he had of being able to support her in the manner she had been accustomed to. On the other hand, his pride made him disdain to shew that he was hurt, or to take any means to prevent the match.[19]

Jack must have been heartbroken as he heard of the preparation for the marriage, including more than 200 guests to be entertained at the bridegroom's house at Kirkby Overblow. The arrangement was that after the wedding at Knaresborough parish church, conducted by the Revd Thomas Collins, the pair would go to breakfast at the Royal Oak, then move on to Kirkby Overblow.

On Sunday, the day before the intended marriage, Jack was riding past Dolly's home – with what anguished thoughts we can well imagine – on his way to the Queen's Head. Suddenly, he realised that a voice – that of a servant girl – was calling to him to turn his horse and ride into the stables of the Royal Oak. There he found Dolly waiting for him. The conversation between them was remembered as follows (with the dialect vowels reinstated). There can be no guarantee of its accuracy after a lapse of more than half a century, but its crucial and emotional nature could have made it an indelible memory, and the account certainly reads convincingly. Slightly reconstructed, it reads as follows:

> 'Well, lass. Thoo's goin' to have a merry day tomorrow. Am I to be the fiddler?'
> 'Thoo never shalt fiddle at my wedding.'
> 'What's the matter? What have Ah done?'
> 'Matters may not end as some folks wish they should... I could wish things to be done another way.'
> 'What? Hadst thoo rather have me? Canst thoo bear starving?'
> 'Aye, lad. With thee I can!'
> 'Give me thy hand then, lass! Skin for skin! It's all done!'[20]

Jack then turned to the servant girl, who was acting as a lookout, and told her that as she and his horse were the only witnesses to this conversation, he would have no hesitation in killing either of them if they divulged his secret. This applied especially to the plan he now suggested to Dolly. That night she was to get ready to leave and place in her window, as a signal that the coast was clear, a lighted candle. This would be seen by a reliable accomplice whom Jack already had in mind.

Dolly now went into the Royal Oak, followed at a discreet interval by Blind Jack, ostensibly having come to express his good wishes to the bride and bridegroom-to-be. He was warmly welcomed by Dickinson and his friends, and joined them in the wonderfully ironic toast: 'Success to the intended couple!'

Jack's next move was to go to the World's End inn – not to be confused with the inn of the same name at Knaresborough – and neither of them, incidentally, anything to do with the supposed Mother Shipton prophecy about the end of the world, but named because of their location at the end or outskirts of a town or village, this particular inn being at the northern end of High Harrogate.[21] At the World's End Jack spoke to the ostler, one of his many good friends, and this man particularly reliable. He told him of his planned elopement with Dolly, asked for his assistance, and even – with his uncanny knowledge of individual horses – asked him to borrow the landlord's mare, whose back he knew to be strong enough to carry two people.

At ten o'clock that night the ostler was waiting for him, with the mare ready-saddled, the two men making secret contact by giving a whistle. They led the two horses – the mare and Jack's own horse – as near as possible to the Royal Oak, not venturing into the paved courtyard for fear the sound of the hooves would be heard. Underneath Dolly's bedroom they waited, Blind Jack anxiously asking his friend, 'Does the star shine in Dolly's window?' Eventually the lighted candle appeared, and Dolly came down to open the door. The story that Jack climbed up a ladder, and helped her out of the bedroom window, is simply a sentimental invention of the fictionalisers. For example: 'Silently he climbed the ladder... He could feel Dolly's sweet breath on his face... (He) helped Dolly onto the ladder, which was no easy feat.'[22]

Metcalf was not going to waste time by using a ladder if his bride-to-be could make her escape through the front door, as she now did. The only problem was that Dolly had to collect some of her many gowns from the adjacent building where her sister slept – and, on that particular night, where the intended bridegroom happened to be sleeping. She got her sister to let her in, and even, with a temerity that Jack would have admired, went into the room where Dickinson was in bed, and picked up a pillion, making the excuse that she must get it brushed and ready for the following morning.[23]

Dolly got safely downstairs and out to the waiting horses – the mare, on which she sat behind the ostler, and Jack on his own horse, leading the way. Old Metcalf does not disclose where they eloped to, simply saying that it involved 'only the trouble of riding 12 miles'. Does this mean the journey there (e.g. to Ripon) or there and back? We do not know which parson he persuaded to marry them – except that we can certainly eliminate the Revd Thomas Collins, who was still expecting to marry Dorothy Benson to Anthony Dickinson the next morning.

But Jack and Dolly were now truly man and wife, and leaving his bride in the security of a friend's house, 5 miles from Harrogate, he rode back to the Queen's Head. He arrived in time to play as usual during the spa-visitors' breakfast, fiddling away as if nothing had happened.

It can safely be assumed that though he said not a word about what he had so brilliantly accomplished, a certain verve and panache in his fiddle-playing would betray the joy of secret triumph. Essentially a man who got things done, he had, in one bold and decisive move, achieved his heart's desire.

Chapter Six

Blind Jack's teapot (see p. 105). (Courtesy of Knaresborough Town Council)

Married Life: The Settled Years

Perhaps not even feeling tired after the excitement and long ride of the previous night, John Metcalf must have been enjoying a rare feeling of satisfaction as he played his breakfast-time melodies for the guests at the Queen's Head. He was, indeed, in a particularly delightful sense, the fiddler at Dolly's wedding – and nothing else seemed to matter.

But what of Dolly's parents, and the man who was that very morning expecting to marry her? He thought of them, just across the Stray there at the Royal Oak. Mrs Benson and her other children would be making sure all was ready for the wedding breakfast, which would be served when the happy couple returned from the ceremony at Knaresborough parish church. He imagined their consternation when they discovered that Dolly was missing. It was not just that she was absent for the wedding, but absent from her home.

Jack did not have long to wait before he knew that the news had broken, and that he was the one suspected of being involved in Dolly's disappearance. A man entered the Queen's Head whose voice Jack instantly recognised. He had been one of the bridegroom's party the previous evening in the Royal Oak. He asked Jack to have a drink with him, something he rarely refused. He accepted, but not wanting their conversation to be overheard, he took this man into a private room, and let him have his say.

'Metcalf,' he said. 'A strange thing has happened since you were with us last night. It concerns Dolly Benson, who was to have been married this morning to Anthony Dickinson – and you are suspected of knowing something about it.' He then described how they were preparing the breakfast while Dickinson went to the church to see Mr Collins. When Dolly did not appear, they first thought she had overslept, then searched through the inn for her, and even dragged the deep well in the fear that she might have fallen in while drawing water for the breakfast. One of Dolly's brothers even rode out to the village of Burton Leonard, about 5 miles to the north of Harrogate, to seek out a young man they knew to have shown a particular interest in Dolly. He declared he knew nothing about the matter, but immediately suggested that Blind Jack might.

Metcalf, who had gone to infinite trouble to keep his liaison with Dolly secret – and in this had had her full cooperation – asked his visitor why on earth he should be suspected. He replied that this man from Burton Leonard had recently been at a dance where Jack was the fiddler, and where, with an observation no doubt made all the keener by his jealousy, he saw Miss Benson, he said:

> …wiping a profuse perspiration from your face with an handkerchief; and this act was accompanied by a look so tender, as left no doubt in his mind of her being strongly attached to you.[1]

Jack at least had in this report something the public could accept as clear evidence that Dolly really was in love with him, and that he had in no sense carried her off against her will. So he decided to admit the truth to Dickinson's friend. He had, he said, since they saw him the previous night, married Dolly, and could only beg pardon of Mr and Mrs Benson. He would not presume to call them father and mother, but wished them to believe that the warmth of this passion for their daughter, together with the despair of ever obtaining their consent, had led him to take these drastic measures. He assured them, however, that he would make 'the best amends in his power by the affectionate conduct he would observe to his wife'. The reaction was hostile:

> The messenger left Metcalf, and reported this declaration to her parents, but they were just as well pleased at it as they would have been at the sight of their building in flames – and, in the height of passion, declared they would put him to death if they met with him.[2]

Two consequences of this elopement are immediately obvious. Firstly, it was sensational news, which must have spread like wildfire amongst the gossiping spa visitors, all of whom had at least heard of the vivacious blind fiddler. Secondly, it was a severe and distressing shock to the Bensons – to say nothing of what it did to the hapless Anthony.

We are told that 'the poor forlorn Dickinson', as soon as he realised what had happened, went off with one of Dolly's brothers to his home at Kirkby Overblow. As they drew near they could hear the church bells ringing in celebration of his supposed wedding. They could even hear them ringing from the church at Harewood, on the other side of the river Wharfe, where Dickinson had previously lived. The unhappy shoemaker was apparently so overcome by what sounded to him like a death knell, that he 'fell from his horse through anguish', and had to be revived before he could explain to the assembled guests that though he had no bride, they were welcome to eat and drink what had been prepared.

The most important part of the fragmentary account of this elopement is the passage which gives an insight into Dorothy Benson's view of young Metcalf and her reason for accepting his impulsive offer of marriage:

> It now became a matter of wonder that she should have preferred a blind man to Dickinson, she being as handsome a woman as any in the county. A lady having asked her why she had refused so many good offers for Blind Jack, she answered, 'Because I could not be happy without him.' And being more particularly questioned, she replied, 'His actions are so singular, and his spirit so manly and enterprising, that I could not help liking him.'[3]

Whether or not these are Dolly's exact words, it seems clear that she had been captivated by Jack's virile personality and his vigorous and original style, and that there is no question that she loved him dearly. Moreover, the love was mutual, and everything suggests that they had a truly happy marriage, one that would be blessed by four children.

No details have survived concerning their first home, except that it was in Knaresborough, where Jack rented 'a small house'. At the end of the Harrogate season one year he managed to buy an old house in Knaresborough, near enough to the Nidd for him to be able to convey stones from the river to the site where the house was rebuilt. The builders, he recalls, gave him an estimate, but he offered them around half the price as a lump sum, which they apparently accepted.

Over the years, true to form, he lived in various houses. Two in the area are traditionally said to be where Blind Jack and his family lived. The first is Red Cat Cottage in the village of Bilton, on the Knaresborough side of Harrogate, which is known to have been held by a 'John Metcalf' in 1778.[4] Around this date, however, (the year of his wife's death) Jack was working in Cheshire, and this may have been another Metcalf. There is much stronger evidence for his having lived in Gate Cottage, a small house on Forest Moor Road just outside Knaresborough with an attractive eighteenth-century interior, which, when sold in 1940, was advertised as having been the home of Blind Jack.[5]

Above: Gate Cottage, Knaresborough.

Below: Blind Jack's home at Spofforth (1792–1810), where he lived in retirement.

Jack continued to travel into Harrogate to play at the Queen's Head and anywhere else where he could earn the money now so necessary to him, and which – for a while, at least – he seems to have spent on his family, and not on gambling. One particular wager, however, that he could not resist was while he was having a drink at the Queen's one day with a butcher. Knowing that Jack carefully avoided the Royal Oak, this butcher bet him that he would not dare go there to pay a visit to his mother-in-law. Jack decided to take him on. He mounted his horse, rode up to the kitchen door of the Royal Oak, and shouted out that he wanted a pint of wine. The servant maids ran upstairs in a fright, particularly as Jack rode his horse into the inn and out through the front door. This was adjudged to be so bold a move that the butcher handed over the money.[6]

The estrangement from Dolly's parents, however, was not to last for long. Jack later paid a serious visit to the inn, asking for Dolly's clothes. He was refused, but on a further visit was handed all he had asked for. This was no doubt because Mrs Benson could no longer suppress her concern for her daughter, who was about to give birth to her first child.

It is unfortunate that a piece of printed misinformation has led to the circulation of an incorrect description of Blind Jack's family. In the semi-fictionalised version of his life by Gary Hogg we are told that Dolly was pregnant with 'the second of four daughters she would present to Jack during their early married life.'[7] This statement that their four children were apparently all girls has naturally been quoted and copied, sometimes with the obvious corollary that nobody in the vast tribe of Metcalfs could claim to be a direct descendant of Blind Jack, because he had no sons! This results from careless reading of the admittedly brief reference made by Jack in 1795. The only way to get at the truth is to consult the Knaresborough Parish Register, where we find the Metcalf births recorded as follows:

Christopher	baptized 7 February 1739
Tabitha	baptized 23 April 1742
Ellen	baptized 18 July 1744
John	baptized 20 March 1746[8]

These dates are interesting, and the first makes the chronology enigmatic. Unless Dolly was already pregnant when they eloped – and there is no hint of this, in contrast to the details of the other woman who had a baby by Jack – this must mean that the marriage had taken place in 1738, when Jack and Dolly were both twenty-one. Yet when his wife died in April 1778 he spoke of their having been married for thirty-nine years – which would improbably place the wedding at the very beginning of 1739, with Dolly in advanced pregnancy. Did his memory fail him here? He says his wife's death was in summer, but the gravestone gives it as 'April 12th'. Although the actual dates, as well as the order of events, are often unclear and confused in Metcalf's own account, we can certainly say, combining it with evidence from the Parish Register, that he and Dolly had two sons and two daughters.

As so often happens in families where there has been a broken relationship, the birth of children now made all the difference. As soon as the first child was born, little Christopher Metcalf, mutual friends persuaded the Bensons to be reconciled to their wayward daughter and rogue of a husband. When the second child, Tabitha, was baptised Mrs Benson actually agreed to be the godmother, and sealed the reconciliation by presenting Jack with the generous sum of twenty guineas.[9]

To give this restless, unpredictable man his due, he seems to have spent the first seven years of his marriage in comparative stability as a reliable breadwinner. His regular sessions as musician at the spa did not in themselves provide sufficient to support his growing family, so he devised a convenient way of supplementing them by using the Queen's Head as a base for what was really Harrogate's first taxi service.

Knowing that many of the spa visitors were too infirm or too lazy to walk to the various wells, and that only the wealthiest had their own carriages, he set up a small service providing a horse-drawn four-wheel chaise, and also a 'one-horse chair' for visitors who wanted to ride from the inns to the wells and back. The idea worked so well that the innkeepers imitated him, providing similar vehicles for hire themselves. So after two seasons he gave up the enterprise.

Gambling was still in his blood, but he seems to have continued to organise races on the Stray, rather than risked money in speculation. One way or another horses were his constant companions, and he was always ready to do a little dealing or hunting. The surest way to earn extra money, he found, was to play his violin at the wealthier country houses. He had an impressive list of gentlemen who were keen to hire him as their musician. In addition to those already mentioned there was a man especially appreciative of his talents, who frequently invited him to bring his violin and oboe to play for his family at his lovely home of Thornville, almost 8 miles east of Knaresborough. He was so well liked here that he lost count of the number of times he came to play, and he was invited for the family Christmas gatherings, year after year, well into his old age. His host was William Thornton, MP and militia enthusiast, one of John Metcalf's most important patrons and supporters. Before long he would be instrumental in initiating Jack into something that would change the whole direction of his life.[10]

As the fees he received for playing at country houses and assemblies were still not a sufficient supplement to his income from the spa, his entreprenurial spirit led him to try to make money in a completely different and surprising way. He decided to become a fishmonger, using contacts he had made while living at his aunt's in Whitby. With several horses at a time he went to the coast, loaded the fish, packed with ice, in the panniers slung across his horses, and transported it back to Yorkshire, taking some to Leeds, and even as far as Manchester.

> So indefatigable was he, that he would frequently walk for two nights and a day with little or no rest; for, as a family was coming on, he was as eager for business as he had been for diversions, still keeping his spirits, as Providence endowed him with good health.[11]

Blind Jack did not leave any details of this remarkable trade in fish – remarkable even for a sighted man – except to relate two episodes during his long and arduous journeys. The first is of how, on the way from Knaresborough to Leeds in a snowstorm, he was crossing a frozen stream when the ice gave way under one of his horses. He found he could not get the horse out until he had removed the two heavy panniers filled with fish. But as soon as the horse was released, it bolted, and galloped back to Knaresborough. Apparently without any assistance, he distributed the weight of the two panniers amongst those carried by his other horses, and continued on his way, reaching Leeds by dawn.[12]

The other episode he recalls is stopping at the Broadstone inn near Halifax. Here he was welcomed by the landlord's son and his friends, who had often visited Harrogate and knew of Blind Jack's exploits as a card player. They invited him to play – at first for liquor, and then for money. At a game of 'shilling whist' Jack won fifteen shillings, and at further

Thornville Royal, Cattal Magna.

games won ten guineas, with an additional shilling for each game, to provide liquor. After careful examination of the pack of cards to make sure there was no cheating, they played on until Jack had won another eight guineas. After treating the players to drinks all round – as well he might – Jack left to return to Knaresborough at ten o'clock that night, all the pack horses except one having been sent on ahead. Crossing the River Wharfe about a mile below Poole, he found the water so deep that he and his horse had to swim across. This experience seems to have been the last straw in a business that, in spite of his toughness and tenacity, had proved a disappointment. This ended his pursuits as a fishmonger, we are told, 'the profits being small, and his fatigue very considerable.'[13]

Profits from his other enterprises, including gambling, were probably no better. It is noticeable that in his memoirs we only read of his successes, rarely of the failures, and the losses which could have been substantial. By the autumn of 1745, when there were already three Metcalf children, and Dolly was pregnant with a fourth, Jack and his family may well have found themselves in straitened circumstances. His only income now was from 'attending Harrogate as a player on the violin in the Long Room'.

Then an opportunity to better himself came from an entirely unexpected quarter. The country was at war. There was a call to arms. The Jacobite rebels under Bonnie Prince Charlie must be stopped at all costs! One of the staunchest patriots in Yorkshire was William Thornton of Thornville Royal, keen enough to raise his own Yorkshire army. And he turned to Blind Jack for help.

Chapter Seven

The 1745 Rebellion: Military Musician

In the closing weeks of the 1745 summer season at Harrogate we can be sure the visitors had more to talk about than their health. The subject of conversation was the Jacobite Rebellion, and the threat it posed to the stability of the country, achieved through the earlier work of Sir Robert Walpole. Now, under George II, the government had little military strength at home, with no barracks and substantial garrisons, and seemed ill-equipped to combat the invasion that had struck in June 1745.

At first this Jacobite incursion must have seemed derisory. Charles Edward Stuart, the Young Pretender to the throne, familiarly known as 'Bonnie Prince Charlie', had landed on the west coast of Scotland with just seven friends. However, he had soon rallied support from the Highlanders, and on 19 August had raised his standard at Glenfinnan. He marched on to Edinburgh, and on 21 September decisively defeated the government forces at the Battle of Prestonpans. He was now preparing to march south, to invade England.

As the English army was under-strength, some felt it essential to raise groups of militia throughout the country, forming an early kind of 'Dad's Army'. One of the most enthusiastic proponents of this was John Metcalf's patron, William Thornton (1712-1769), a gentleman very much involved in local affairs. As well as later being MP for York (1747-54 and 1758-61), he was a justice of the peace and free citizen of York.[1] In 1758, he would at Thornville Royal interrogate the Knaresborough schoolmaster, Eugene Aram, before sending him to be tried in York, where he was hanged for murder the following year. He would well remember the disappearance of Aram's victim, the Knaresborough shoemaker, Daniel Clark, in the February of 1745. Indeed, one reason that the crime was not solved in that year may have been that there was so much preoccupation with the Jacobite Rebellion.[2] A long poem in fulsome praise of Thornton, published in *The Gentleman's Magazine*, has been attributed to Aram.[3]

The threat from the rebels was becoming so serious that a general county meeting, addressed by William Thornton, was held at York Castle. Here he expressed his opinion that a militia of 4,000 men should be raised in support of the King's regular army. He claimed that to pay for recruitment, provision of uniforms, arms and food, he already had a subscription list promising £90. When his proposal failed to receive a majority vote, Thornton decided he would go it alone, and form a smaller company of soldiers at his own expense – soon to be known as the Yorkshire Blues.[4]

He made a start by coming to Knaresborough on 1 October 1745. One of his best contacts, through whom he could reach and recruit working men, was John Metcalf. So he invited him to his Knaresborough inn, plied him liberally with punch, and then put his case to him.

Did he realise, he asked him, what a grave danger now confronted the nation? Did he know that the rebels in Scotland were soon to be joined by the French, and that unless they were vigorously opposed would invade England, and 'violate our wives, daughters and sisters'?[5] Would he therefore be willing to join the new company of soldiers he was about to raise? John Metcalf, who was not only a proud Yorkshireman, but fiercely patriotic, immediately replied that he would indeed like to join. But what use would he be as a blind man?

Thornton believed that, far from being useless, Metcalf could initiate and motivate the whole project. He was a man of the people, well known in the district through his sporting, gambling and general conviviality. Did he not know 'of any spirited fellows who were likely to make good soldiers?' Jack replied that he certainly did, and so, as assistant to an experienced sergeant Thornton had already appointed, he was given the job of organising a recruitment drive.

The next day he went round Knaresborough and the adjacent villages, giving a rattle on his drum, perhaps, then playing a martial tune on his oboe, followed by an impassioned appeal for men to join the new army. How promising he made it sound! It was only going to be a short campaign to drive out the rebels, and would result in either military promotion, or in being paid off handsomely by the government. The general feeling of outrage at the Jacobite rebellion, combined with Blind Jack's powers of persuasion, resulted in many men volunteering to serve, including wagoners, carpenters and artificers – men with the technical skills Thornton knew he would need for transporting and setting up tents, building bridges, repairing weapons and so forth.

The recruitment went so well that within two days Blind Jack and the sergeant had enlisted 140 men. William Thornton had now no need to look elsewhere or try to recruit from other parts of Yorkshire. Moreover, since he could form his company from volunteers in a particular area, the new soldiers would have much in common and a higher morale – an anticipation, I would think, of the experience in the First World War, when a great sense of comradeship was engendered when men came along with their friends to enlist in local groups of volunteers, such as the Bradford Pals, the Sheffield Pals and so on. It was later said that Thornton's volunteers turned out to be better in behaviour and morale than the usual regular soldiers.[6]

Captain Thornton, as he was now being styled, having been commissioned by the anti-rebel North Riding Association, found himself the victim of success in the recruitment drive so vigorously undertaken by Blind Jack. He had agreed to take these men on at five shillings on enlistment (five times more than the traditional 'King's Shilling'), and then pay them a shilling a day while in his service. Realising that he could not afford this for so many, especially as he had no idea how long the campaign would last, he decided that it would be realistic to reduce the number to sixty-four privates.

How did Thornton make his selection of the best? With the sergeant he would watch how the men responded to orders, assess their speed in running, and their stamina in marching long distances. Blind Jack would question them about their background and experience. Could they use their fists – and firearms – for example? Had they worked away from home before? And to test their strength, he might run his experienced fingers over their muscles.

Captain Thornton's next step was to order from Leeds good-quality cloth to be made into uniforms for these men. The coats were blue, trimmed and faced with buff, and with buff waistcoats. The predominant colour of blue, distinct from that of the commonly seen redcoats, was what give their name, 'The Yorkshire Blues' – though, as was the custom, the company was officially named after the commanding officer, and also known as 'Thornton's'.

Thornton wanted the uniforms for his picked men as soon as possible, which meant that the tailors would have to work on Sunday. They at first refused, saying that this was breaking the Sabbath. But the captain successfully communicated his sense of urgency. He rebuked their fanatical scruples in these words: 'You rascals! If your houses were on fire, would you not be glad to extinguish the flames on a Sunday?'[7]

Was there a uniform for Blind Jack? A particularly splendid one, in fact, distinguished by gold braid. This befitted the man Captain Thornton now invited to be his military musician, employed to lead the troops on the march, and even into battle, by playing, especially his oboe, and sometimes his fiddle, beating on a drum, and encouraging them to join in the popular patriotic songs.

To leave his little family and pregnant wife cannot have been easy, but he no doubt argued that here was an opportunity not to be missed and that, before long, when they had put the rebels to rout, he would be back with a useful sum of money. There was also the possibility of military glory, and Dolly must have been proud to see him on parade, as a kind of non-commissioned officer, wearing a braided tricorn hat, intended to show he was a cut above the ordinary foot-soldiers:

> All matters being adjusted, the company was drawn up, and amongst them Blind Jack made no small figure, being near six feet two inches high and, like his companions, dressed in blue and buff, with a large gold-laced hat. So well pleased was the captain with his appearance that he said he would give an hundred guineas for one eye to stick in the head of his dark champion.[8]

The training of these raw recruits would have been reduced to a few essentials. We can imagine them, appropriately based in the grounds of the ruined Knaresborough Castle, being drilled by the sergeant, and shown how to handle muskets, a consignment of which, with a supply of ball and powder, Captain Thornton had arranged to be sent from the Tower of London. They would also have been taught, not only how to load, aim and fire, but how to fix to the musket the long, stabbing blade of a bayonet, and use it against the enemy.

As soon as this basic training was completed, Captain Thornton marched his men off to Thornville, leaving Knaresborough in style, with their smartly dressed musician at their head, playing on his oboe military marches of the day, such as 'Lillibulero' or 'The British Grenadiers'. During a further period of training at Thornville the captain liberally supplied them with meals of roast ox, washed down with the best beer, seven years old. Then he finally lined up his company, which would amount to seventy or so, including at least one lieutenant and sergeant, his ensign and his musician, and addressed them as follows:

> My lads... You are going to form part of a ring-fence to the finest estate in the world! The King's army is on its march to the northward – and I have the pleasing confidence that you are all willing to join them.

They replied, as if one soul animated them:

> We will follow you to the world's end![9]

We might imagine that Blind Jack, when he heard – and joined in with – those last words, could hardly resist thinking he would rather interpret them as marching off to one of his favourite pubs in High Harrogate. But, suitably inspired, the Yorkshire Blues now marched off northwards, Jack striking up with 'a march of the captain's choosing'.

They first marched to Boroughbridge, where they joined the forces of General George Wade, in overall command of the King's armies in the north. Only two years earlier he had been promoted to field marshal, and his chief claim to fame was in successfully defeating the Scottish clansmen in the earlier Jacobite uprising of 1715. What really interested Blind

Jack was the fact that General Wade had helped to control the Scottish Highlands by constructing (between 1726 and 1737) excellent roads through the remotest countryside. Jack's admiration for this senior officer must have been a contributory factor in his own interest in road building.

The general ordered Captain Thornton to move towards Newcastle, scouring the countryside on the way, to make sure that the rebels had not already infiltrated, or were roaming about as stragglers. There seems to have been no action, but plenty of marching over the moors, Blind Jack leading the way. When they rested for the night, quartered in various villages, the captain always insisted on Jack being with him to entertain his guests by playing and singing. More than entertainment, his contribution helped to maintain the patriotic fervour provoked by the invading Jacobites. Only one song title is mentioned, but this gives a good idea of a popular feeling in 1745. Another sea shanty, like 'Tit for Tat', this is the rousing 'Britons, strike home'! Although it has a naval subject, this song was especially popular with English soldiers and had been included in 'The Beggars' Opera' in 1729, originally having been a tune in Purcell's opera 'Bonduca'. It tells of a woman so in love with her man that she follows him on board a warship:

> The press-gang they took him, my joy and my pride,
> And, dressed in boy's clothing, I fought by his side.

Out of 900 sailors on board, 500 were slain in a sea battle. Both she and her boyfriend were wounded, but lived to be married. Though the song is about war at sea, its chorus serves as a general call to British people to hit the enemy hard:

> Come, all you bold seamen, and see what is done,
> See how a brave woman will fight for a man
> So we'll cross the salt seas, let the wind blow so strong,
> While our rakish young fellows cry
> 'Britons, strike home, boys,
> Britons, strike home!'[10]

These must have been the words that Blind Jack actually sang, 'in a good voice', as well as making the most of the lively tune on oboe and fiddle. He had a considerable audience, mainly composed of Captain Thornton's friends and other officers, who were so pleased with him that they 'frequently offered him money, but this he always refused, knowing that his acceptance of it would displease his commander'.[11]

When they reached Newcastle the general issued orders for the Yorkshire Blues to attach themselves to Pulteney's Regiment, named after their commandant, General Harry Pulteney (1686-1767). This regiment he considered to be in great need of reinforcement because it had recently suffered many casualties in action abroad.[12] After a circuitous march of perhaps a hundred miles, 'Thornton's' were glad to settle down for a while, camping near 'Pulteney's' on Newcastle Moor, where the captain had arranged for tents to be set up for his men. As the start of a bitterly cold winter was now being felt, he issued blankets for each tent, and typical of the contrast between eighteenth-century officers and their men, procured for himself a large and comfortable marquee, the furnishings of which alone (according to Metcalf) cost eighty guineas.

Thornton made sure that Blind Jack was housed in the tent next to his marquee. The musician was now so well in with his captain that he was bold enough to joke with him that the men, newly installed in their tents, were entitled to a housewarming. Thornton asked him how much he would need to give them all a drink. Jack had the answer ready: 'Three shillings a tent'. The captain, who seemed at the time to have had ample cash to dispense, not only agreed to pay this, but also produced ten guineas to pay for drinks all round in the adjacent camp. Realising this was an opportunity for his men to forge a good relationship with the soldiers they had just joined, he explained to Jack: 'As you join Pulteney's Regiment they will smell your breath!'[13]

The housewarming drink was well-timed. That very night it started to snow, and soon there was a depth of 6in on the bleak moorland. They would have gladly stayed put in their tents, but after only a week they were ordered to strike camp, and prepare to march out through the deepening snow towards Hexham, about 15 miles to the west. This was because General Wade had received intelligence that the rebels had crossed the border and would soon cross Hadrian's Wall.

The order was that they should leave Newcastle at daybreak, but the vanguard of Swiss mercenaries refused to get ready at this early hour, and the army did not leave until 10.30 a.m. Conditions were severe, with hail and hard frost, and the snow so deep that in places the pioneers had to dig a way through for the artillery and the baggage carts. It took them about four hours to cover 7 miles and reach the village of Ovington, only halfway to Hexham. There, at ten o'clock, they tried to pitch their tents in the dark, but the ground was so hardened by the frost that very few tent-pegs could be driven in, and most of the men slept in the open in the abundance of straw that had been provided.

At eleven o'clock Captain Thornton left the camp with his lieutenant and rode on to Hexham, ostensibly to buy provisions for his men, but also to spend the night in comfort with his relation, Sir Edward Blacket.[14] In the morning, although it was a Sunday, orders had been given for the company to march on. It was the normal custom to pile up the straw they had used for bedding and make a great bonfire of it, so they could have a good warm before their departure. However, orders had been given that the straw should be left there, in case they needed it on their return.

Blind Jack, sensing that the miserably cold men were in a low state of morale, decided to disobey orders, and, in typical fashion, took the initiative. Overruling the sergeant, he called out that they should go ahead and follow the custom: 'My lads,' he said. 'Get the straw together and burn it. Our captain will pay for more if we should want it.' The men quickly responded, and as soon as the fire was blazing away, Jack took his fiddle and played for them as they danced all round it. Captain Thornton and his lieutenant rode up, astonished to see this merrymaking round the leaping flames. But although orders had been disobeyed, the officers were delighted to see the men in such high spirits, the better able to continue their dreary march through the snow.[15]

With the rest of General Wade's army they reached Hexham at last. After three days the general left them to return to Newcastle, and then marched south to secure Yorkshire. It had been learnt that the rebels had invaded England almost unopposed, but were moving down the western side, afraid to confront the troops of the famous General Wade. Their threat was increasingly serious. By the beginning of December they had entered Derby, and would have moved on to London if Bonnie Prince Charlie had not been forced, by the overwhelming opinion of his officers, alarmed at the overstretched lines of communication, to withdraw northwards on 6 December.

Talk amongst the Yorkshire Blues, still at Hexham, was now of the new commander-in-chief, who was to make it his business to defeat the Jacobite rebels. He was William Augustus, Duke of Cumberland, second son of George II. The Yorkshire volunteers would learn from their contact with the regulars of Pulteney's Regiment something of the duke's military career. Though aged only twenty-five, he had much experience in the field, had been wounded at the Battle of Dettingen and been narrowly defeated by the French at Fontenoy only the previous May. He was now driven by a determination to defeat the pro-French rebels and bring credit to his father. Himself a military man, George II had the distinction of being the last British monarch to lead his troops into battle.

The duke's army caught up with the rebels as they moved back towards Scotland, engaging them on the border of Westmorland. His 300 dragoons dismounted and advanced, but were driven back by the superior musketry of the Jacobites, who were able to make an orderly retreat to Penrith. The King's army pursued them from there to Carlisle Castle, where they easily held out. On Christmas Day 1745, the duke received a present of artillery, ordered from Whitehaven, and by the 30 December his bombardment had caused the rebel garrison to surrender.

The duke temporarily returned to London and handed over his command to General Henry Hawley. It was he who was now to take the battle further north, facing the rebels on their own ground. With additional troops withdrawn from the Netherlands, he ordered the King's army to march on Scotland. And this included Captain Thornton's Yorkshire Blues, soon to have their first taste of the chaotic horror of war.

Chapter Eight

Into Battle: Prisoner of the Rebels

In the first freezing days of 1746 the armies of Lieutenant-General Hawley were entering Scotland and marching on Edinburgh. As the main body of the rebel Highlanders was encamped at Torwood, roughly halfway between Falkirk and Stirling, the English army moved in this direction, pitching their tents on the north-east side of Falkirk on 16 January.

Amongst the King's troops were Pulteney's Regiment, with the Yorkshire Blues attached to them, still led not only by Captain William Thornton, but also their redoubtable musician, Blind Jack. He had kept up their spirits on the long march from Hexham – a distance of well over a hundred miles over difficult terrain. Now he was to be involved in some real action with the enemy, and though he was not an eyewitness in the literal sense, he heard everything for himself and remembered all that was said to him by his fellow soldiers who were eyewitnesses. Even though his account was not dictated until he was in his late seventies, he would have told the story again and again, and even if he told it, like Shakespeare's soldier, 'with advantages', its substantial accuracy can be confirmed by other attempts to reconstruct the battle. Blind Jack's testimony, in fact, remains one of the most convincing and vivid pieces of material in the annals of the Jacobite Rebellion.

The first thing he noted was that although they were camped about 3 miles from the enemy, it was close enough on the first night for the Yorkshire lads to see their lights in the distance. In the morning the pickets from the advanced lookout positions came back to report that they had seen no sign of activity in the Jacobite camp and that there was no likelihood of an attack. A later report said that their flags had been seen as they moved towards Stirling – an apparent indication of retreat. This gave General Hawley – who should have suspected that this was a tactical ruse – a false sense of security. He ordered his troops to stand easy and 'to pile their arms'. Then he went off to take breakfast with Lady Kilmarnock at Callendar House.

Meanwhile the rebels, whose flags had been a decoy, marched north and entered a hidden valley close to the position of the King's forces. They were spotted by one of the locals, a Lowlander, one of many others loyal to King George – and he ran into the English camp to give the alert:

> 'Gentleman! What are you about? The Highlanders will be upon you!'
> On which some of the officers said, 'Seize that rascal! He is spreading a false alarm.'
> 'Will you, believe your own eyes?' replied the man, when instantly the truth of his assertion became apparent.[1]

Seeing that the enemy – under the overall command of Lord George Murray – were advancing towards them, the English reacted swiftly, drums beating, men rushing to grab their arms and get into formation. General Hawley was eventually summoned from his relaxation, arriving in such haste that he left his hat behind. In the late afternoon of Friday 17 January 1746, the Battle of Falkirk was under way.

Captain Thornton had always intended that his Yorkshire Blues should be in the forefront of the battle, but to his great disappointment, although they were attached to Pulteney's Regiment in the first rank, he was ordered to advance in a less prominent position, in

Young Blind Jack leading the Yorkshire Blues into battle. (Peter Kearney)

support of the 'matrosses', or foot soldiers with the artillery.[2] So, from his horse, Thornton urged on his men, as they marched on rising ground, against the wind and heavy rain, to face the Jacobites. They were a small but important part of a complex first line, consisting (from the left) as they advanced, of the dragoons of Hamilton, Ligonier and Cobham, the regiments of Wolfe, Cholmondeley, Pulteney, Price, Ligonier and the Royals. This meant that the Yorkshire Blues were near the centre and likely to feel the brunt of rebel onslaught.[3] Marching at the head of his Yorkshire friends from Knaresborough and district was their blind musician, playing a brisk tune on his oboe, with its sharp, trumpet-like sound, his courageous example modestly summarised by the single line:

Metcalf played before them to the field.[4]

Captain Thornton now had another disappointment. The flag-cannon, which should have been in the lead, became stuck, its wheels sinking into the boggy moorland. Furiously shouting, 'Damn this accident! We shall see no sport today!', Thornton left his men with the captain of the train, so they could try to free and move forward the artillery, while he rode on into the enemy lines, along with horsemen from the regiments of Hamilton and Gardner, who had apparently been placed in the front line to atone for their poor conduct at the Battle of Prestonpans.[5]

Blind Jack would not have minded being left with the cannon and the horses that pulled them. Though prepared to fight, he could not, in the confusion of battle, have been sure whether he was fighting friend or foe. Here, at least, he was able to use his experience to calm the horses, terrified by the sound of the enemy musketry. Only a short distance away he could hear the murderous cries and curses of battle – and think that his captain was now in the thick of it.

As soon as the English cavalry got within range of the Highlanders, they were met with a volley of musket fire. Instead of reloading, the rebels threw down their muskets and took out their pistols, firing into the heads of the horses at close range. This not only played havoc with the cavalry, but also caused terrible disruption and panic amongst the ranks of English infantry all along the lines, with the wounded horses running wildly amongst them. As they retreated, the Highlanders came on in hot pursuit, cutting the English down with their broadswords. The appalling situation was summed up in a remark that Blind Jack later remembered having heard uttered by one of the men: 'Dear brethren! We shall all be massacred this day!'

As the ferocious Jacobites drew near to the group of cannon, and the Yorkshire Blues and matrosses struggling to move them, the captain of the train gave orders for all the horses to be cut free so they could join in the general retreat. They might all indeed have been massacred, but were saved by the sudden intervention of General Huske, who had brought up three regiments of infantry, and was now engaging the Highlanders on their left flank. This did nothing to save the day, however, and General Hawley had been forced into a retreat in which he left behind seven cannon, and all his baggage, stores and tents. Hundreds of English soldiers and officers were killed, wounded or captured – and one estimate claims that 300 dragoons were killed by the Highlanders' opening volley. The Prince's army, on the other hand, is thought to have lost only fifty dead and eighty wounded.[6]

Blind Jack managed to escape from the battlefield along with forty-eight of the Yorkshire Blues, the rest having been taken prisoner. He had no idea what had happened to his captain, but – ever mindful of equestrian concerns – he decided that he could at least try to secure two of the horses which Thornton had left at a house near Falkirk. The same evening he found his way there and spoke to the woman of the house, who had previously been a supporter of King George. Now, having heard that the King's forces had been defeated at Falkirk, she had switched her allegiance to Bonnie Prince Charlie, saying 'the defeat of George's folk was a just judgement'. Still, she allowed Jack to go to the stable and saddle the horses. He was leading out the first, when he found himself surrounded by a few stragglers from the Jacobite army. They told him they wanted the horse. When Jack refused, they simply said they would shoot him. As soon as he heard them cock their muskets, he, like the woman, decided it would be prudent to change sides. When they told him they wanted the horse for Prince Charles, he handed it over with feigned pleasure, and later left with the other horse.

As he was doing so he heard a voice he recognised – that of Snowden, who was Captain Thornton's coachman. He told Jack that the last he had seen of the captain was when he was riding towards the enemy lines, and that he feared he had been killed. The two roamed about the boggy district, making enquiries, then caught up with the retreating army. But nobody could tell them what had happened to Captain Thornton, who was regarded as missing, presumed killed in action. Jack let the coachman take charge of the horse, and walked with the cold and weary defeated men as far as Linlithgow. The next day they formed up and marched in a more orderly fashion on to Edinburgh. Here they found that the news of the Highlanders' victory at Falkirk had changed the allegiance of the crowds from King George to Prince Charles Edward Stuart, who was now destined, it seemed, to become the rightful British monarch.[7]

The defeated army gradually reassembled in camps on the outskirts of Edinburgh. Metcalf remembers how dispirited the Yorkshire Blues were at this time. They had lost twenty of their men as prisoners of the rebels, and in addition to their captain, they had lost two other officers, the lieutenant and the ensign. It was Captain Thornton they missed most, because he was so greatly respected for the way he had always given care and attention to his men.

One day Blind Jack was summoned to the headquarters near the abbey. A group of senior officers were trying to find out what had happened to Captain Thornton, and were also curious about the blind musician he had brought from Yorkshire. Implying that these Yorkshire Blues did not seem to have put up much of a resistance, the first question was about how he, with all his disadvantages, had been able to escape from the battlefield, along with the others. Jack knew that the question had been put by one of the officers of the dragoons, some of whom had ignominiously galloped away from the enemy. So he answered:

I found it very easy – by following the sound of the dragoons' horses. They made such a clatter on the stones!

When the laughter from the other officers had subsided, a more serious question was put to Metcalf by Colonel Cockayne, the officer commanding Pulteney's Regiment. He asked him how, blind as he was, he had dared to venture on military service, with all its unseen hazards and dangers. Blind Jack gave the reply:

If I had possessed a pair of good eyes, sir, I would never have come here to risk the loss of them by gunpowder![8]

Jack gave a bow and excused himself, then returned to the despondent men of the Yorkshire Blues, personally feeling frustrated and annoyed that nothing had been established about the fate of Captain Thornton, nor any effort made to go in search of him.

As it happened, Thornton had survived, and had joined several other officers scattered around the outskirts of Falkirk, trying to make the best of things. According to the account he later gave Blind Jack, he managed to find a house, where a Royalist Scotswoman gave him shelter. While he was in front of the fire, drying his uniform, soaked by the heavy rain during the battle, he heard the sound of bagpipes at the door. Jacobite soldiers had come to requisition the house and use it as their headquarters.

The captain rushed upstairs and hid behind a bedroom door while they searched the rooms. Then the woman of the house came up and silently took him to a tiny closet, only a yard and a half square. He went inside, and she moved a dresser in front of the door, and piled it high with dishes. Ten minutes later a number of important Highland officers arrived, including Lord George Murray, one of Bonnie Prince Charlie's finest commanders and closest advisors, but whose advice he did not often accept.[9]

Curled up in the closet, Thornton was in a wretched state, shivering with cold in his still-wet clothes, and soon coughing so much that the woman feared he would be heard by the officers who had taken over the adjoining bedrooms. However, she managed to keep him going by slipping food and drink through a gap in the bottom of the door. By the Monday night the captain was in such a state that he called to the woman saying that he was determined to come out, whatever the consequences, 'for I will not die like a dog in this hole.'[10]

She persuaded him to stay there until the following night, when she enlisted the help of an old carpenter who was loyal to King George. He removed the dresser, liberated the cramped captain, and helped him down to the woman's apartment, where she gave him hot tea. Then dressed him in 'a pladdie and brogues' and a black wig, and gave him a bag of tools, so he could look like the carpenter's assistant.[11] They slipped out of the house as soon as it was light, Captain Thornton thanking the woman for her loyalty and timely help, and giving her eight of the ten guineas he still had about him. The other two he gave to the carpenter who put them in his mouth in case he was searched. Another detail which gives this story an authentic touch is the Scots dialect Metcalf quotes being used by the carpenter when in the crowds of rebel soldiers he thought they might be suspicious of the one supposed to be his assistant. 'Come along, ye filthy loon!', he said. 'Ye've had half a bannock and a mutchkin of drink in yer wame. We shall be too late for our day's work!'[12]

They soon found themselves going over the ground where the battle had taken place and Captain Thornton could not help commenting: 'Yonder's the place where such a sad piece of work was made of it on Friday last'.[13] After managing to avoid a great crowd of rebel soldiers who had been plundering Callendar House, they reached the home of one of the carpenter's friends, where the captain was given an egg to eat, cooked in the peat ashes, and then moved on to another house, where he found a horse, and from there rode safely back to Edinburgh.

Unaware of Thornton's adventures, and thinking he might be able to do something to help his captain, Jack decided he must make an effort to find him. His stratagem was to contact a man from Knaresborough who happened to be a supporter of the rebels. Telling him that he was disillusioned with the defeated King's army, he said he was going to offer his services as a musician to Prince Charles. This man told him that they were sending an Irishman, one of their spies, to see the Prince at Falkirk, and that Metcalf could go with him.

They got past the sentries and reached Linlithgow, where they spent the night at the Exchange House. The next morning a party of Jacobite soldiers came in to drink whiskey. One of them dropped a small silver-mounted pistol, which the Irishman picked up from the floor after they left. He offered it to Blind Jack, who handled it, but refused it, saying it would not do to have it about him if he was searched.

By another of those curious coincidences that so often appear in Blind Jack's narrative, he met a woman at Linlithgow who asked him to take a small package to her husband – who happened to be Lord George Murray's cook. Even the man she used to guide him there was a horse-dealer who knew of Metcalf through having frequented horse fairs in Yorkshire. On reaching the house in Falkirk (the house from which Thornton had escaped four hours earlier) Blind Jack found the cook and he actually claims that he was then introduced to Lord George Murray himself, who chatted with him and invited him to share a single glass of wine with him. The wine was very scarce, Jack recalled, because both the rebels and the English had made use of the house and 'swept the cupboard clean of its crumbs.'[14]

Jack now moved through the snow to the market place in Falkirk, crowded with Jacobite soldiers. He was looked at with suspicion, partly because he was still wearing the coat of blue, faced with buff, that some recognised as one of the Royalist uniforms. He told them that he had been playing his fiddle for the English officers, one of whom had given him the coat from a soldier who was killed in the battle. Still hoping to hear something of Captain Thornton, he continued with his pretence that he was going to offer his services as a musician to the Prince.

By yet another coincidence – this time an unfortunate one – he was recognised in the market place by a man who had seen him in Harrogate, and knew of his reputation. Soon Jack found himself surrounded by rebel soldiers, arrested, and taken to the nearest guard room. Here they searched him to see if he was carrying any letters. All they found on him was a pack of cards, which they proceeded to split with a razor, in case they contained hidden messages. He was then taken up into a makeshift prison in the loft, where he was confined along with several other prisoners, including a dragoon who had been captured at the disastrous battle five days earlier.[15]

After three days in this wretched prison, with the snow and bitterly cold air coming in through the roof, Blind Jack was brought down to face a Jacobite court martial. With his usual confidence and plausibility, he succeeded in convincing the court, his fiddle still in his hand, that he really was trying to offer his services as musician to Bonnie Prince Charlie. They let him go, and even helped him on his way. He needed to get a clean shirt, he said, from Linlithgow, but dare not go there because he was afraid of encountering 'George's devils'. So they offered him safe conduct in the company of the Irish spy. After 2 miles on their journey they met an English officer, who told them that Captain Thornton had just got back to Edinburgh. They set off for the city themselves, where Jack went straight to the captain, and there was mutual rejoicing that both were safe and well.

When Thornton told his story, and explained that he was still dressed in the rough clothes of a carpenter's mate, and had no money whatever, the resourceful Jack went off to find a friend, from whom he borrowed £30: 'Tailors were instantly set to work', he recalls. 'And next morning the captain was enabled to visit his brother officers at the abbey'.[16] It is recorded elsewhere that contemporaries thought that Thornton had 'behaved very gallantly' at the Battle of Falkirk.[17]

For the next week or so the King's army rested and licked its wounds. Lieutenant-General Henry Hawley's campaign had been an utter disaster. But now everything was to change. The Yorkshire Blues, like the rest of the army, must have taken heart when they heard that the Duke of Cumberland had arrived in Edinburgh, eager to resume command.

Chapter Nine

The Battle of Culloden, 16 April 1746

William Augustus, Duke of Cumberland, arrived in Edinburgh on 30 January 1746. He apprised himself of the general situation and two days later rode at the head of the army as they marched towards Falkirk.

Captain Thornton was clearly on good terms with the duke, who took an interest in the Yorkshire Blues, and expressed his admiration of the way their blind musician was able to keep such good step to the regulation drum beat requiring seventy-five paces to the minute.

> His Royal Highness took notice of Metcalf, and spoke to him several times on the march, observing how well, by the sound of the drum, he was able to keep his pace.[1]

His interest in him later led to the remarkable fact that Blind Jack of Knaresborough was one of the few people – perhaps the only one – to have had close social contact with mighty protagonists on opposing sides of the Jacobite Rebellion, namely, Lord George Murray and the Duke of Cumberland.

When the army reached Linlithgow they expected an attack from the rebels, and the duke ordered the regiments to be drawn up in formation. Riding between the battle lines he addressed his troops, according to Blind Jack, as follows:

> If there be any who think themselves in a bad cause, or are afraid to engage, thinking they might fight against any of their relations, let them now turn out, receive pardon, and go about their business, without any further question.[2]

The soldiers replied by giving the duke three hearty 'huzzahs', and nobody apparently availed themselves of the opportunity to leave. In the event, there was no confrontation with the enemy at this point. The intelligence about their resistance proved false. They had, in fact, withdrawn from Falkirk, to where the English army now proceeded without hindrance, later following the Jacobites northwards, marching up through Stirling, Perth, Brechin, Montrose and Stonehaven – and finally to Aberdeen.

Here they spent the rest of the winter waiting for the snow to clear from the roads over the Highlands and for the River Spey to be sufficiently fordable for this large army to cross. The duke used this time to give the infantry more training, in particular, teaching them how to use their bayonets against the arms of the rebels, when they came at them holding up their protective 'targets' – small round leather shields. The order now was that each man should strike at the enemy immediately to his right. Blind Jack's reference to this fits in exactly with other observations about the new tactics that had been learnt after the defeats of Prestonpans and Falkirk.[3]

The duke also sought to keep up morale by organising social events for the officers and their wives, including local ladies supportive of King George. Not long before they left Aberdeen on the long march to Culloden, the duke decided to organise a ball. It was a brave show, some of the enemy camps being only 20 miles away. For this reason, in order to minimise the chances of a surprise attack, he gave orders that no invitations or details were to be sent out until five o'clock, even though the ball was to start at six. He was aware that Colonel Howard's Old Buffs had a small band of wind instruments, but the players were German, and not familiar with music for English country dancing. So he asked Captain Thornton if he could borrow his excellent fiddler. One of the happiest of Blind Jack's memories must have been this occasion when he was privileged to play for the duke, his officers and their womenfolk, raising their spirits as a prelude to one of the most famous battles in English history:

> Twenty-five couples danced for eight hours, and his Royal Highness made one of the set; and several times, as he passed Metcalf, who stood on a chair to play, he shouted 'Thornton's, play up.' But Jack needed no exhortation, for he was very well practised, and better inclined.[4]

Playing until two o'clock in the morning would not have been all that unusual for Blind Jack. Later that day he received from the duke a tip of two guineas. He checked with the captain to see if it was permissible to accept this as a serving soldier. Thornton said that it was, but thought it might be tactful to treat the duke's three servants – the valet, cook and groom, who came round for a party that night, the captain providing them with plenty of additional drink.

Satisfied with the accuracy of intelligence that Bonnie Prince Charlie and his Highlanders were now based at Inverness, the Duke of Cumberland gave orders for the King's army to march to the north and west as soon as weather permitted. They set out on this journey of at least a hundred miles on 8 April 1746.

The long march of those troops, with cavalry and artillery, was an impressive feat, carefully organised by the duke, who arranged for no fewer than 225 kettledrums to be beaten throughout the journey, to guarantee a steady pace.[5] The Yorkshire Blues, and other soldiers within earshot, had the additional stimulus of Blind Jack's music, alternating between the sound of his fiddle and his oboe.

The march was made easier by the roads laid down by General Wade for the very purpose of better military control of rebellious areas. By 1735 he had built 250 miles of road, and forty bridges. As John Metcalf marched through the wilds of Scotland, we can be sure that he appreciated the sound surfaces of the roads, with their camber designed to drain off water into the ditches at each side. Here he had a fine example to inspire his own later road building.

Three days after their departure the King's army reached Cullen on the coast, to the north-west. Here they were joined by the Earl of Albemarle's six battalions of infantry, and two regiments of cavalry (he was later to command the front line at Culloden), and General Mordaunt's reserve of three battalions and three guns.[6] Considerably strengthened, the duke's army crossed the River Spey on 14 April. They had expected opposition from the 2,000 rebels under Lord John Drummond, who had been guarding the river. But these withdrew on the approach of outmatching Royalist numbers – now totalling nearly 9,000 men.

Once across the river, they marched without opposition to reach Nairn the following day, 15 April. As this was the duke's twenty-fifth birthday he took the opportunity (parallel to his having organised a ball for the officers) of raising the morale of the rank and file by issuing an extra ration of cheese, and supplying all ranks with brandy – each regiment being issued with two gallons. The duke was certainly popular with his men, not only because of treats like this, but because he had, during the march, dismounted, and walked part of the way with them on foot.

Whilst morale was high in the King's forces, the Highlanders were exhausted, ill-fed and dejected. But on 14 April, inspired by the sound of the pipes, they marched out of Inverness to Drummossie Moor, 5 miles to the east, where they camped near Culloden House, soon to give its name to the battle.[7] On 15 April, the day their enemies were celebrating the duke's birthday, the Jacobites attempted a surprise night attack, but failed, and had to retreat to Culloden. In the early hours of 16 April, Prince Charles consulted Lord George Murray, who advised him either to return to Inverness or disperse his men into the safety of the Highlands. If he insisted on fighting the King's army, said Murray, he must move to a better position, because a battle on Drummossie Moor would mean defeat.[8] The Prince, once again, did not accept his advice, but decided to take a stand at Culloden, and face the advancing army.

A curious gap in John Metcalf's narrative, or perhaps an omission by his editor, is the absence of any details of what happened to him and the men from Yorkshire at Culloden. In contrast to what he says about the Battle of Falkirk, there is only a paragraph about how the army 'engaged the rebels on Culloden Moor', with a comment about how the infantry used their bayonets to attack the Highlanders coming at them with their targets and broadswords, and also how Kingston's Light Horse made their spectacular charge.[9]

This does not mean, however, that the Yorkshire Blues, with Captain Thornton and his musician, were not present. There is plenty of evidence that Pulteney's Regiment, to which the forty-eight remaining men were still attached, were very much involved in the Battle of Culloden, and were, in fact, eventually in the first rank facing the rebels. From the left, the line-up of regiments was as follows: Barrell's, Munro's, Royal Scots Fusiliers, Campbell's, Price's, Cholmondeley's, St Clair's Royal Scots, and Pulteney's.[10] The fact that they were moved up to this position on the extreme right flank fits in well with Blind Jack having noted the charge of Kingston's cavalry, who had formed up next to them.

It would be an exaggeration to say that Blind Jack actually fought at Culloden, except in the limited sense that he presumably marched and played at the head of the men when they took up their position with Pulteney's Regiment – as he had done at Falkirk. He would be in considerable danger, and was an important aural witness – but if he had done any actual hand-to-hand fighting with the Highlanders, we would surely have heard about it. His most important contribution to the King's cause was essentially his encouragement of the men by his formidable presence and his music on the battlefield – an important counterpart to the persistent sound of the rebels' bagpipes.

The two armies came within sight of each other at about eleven o'clock, and soon had lined up with only about 300 yards between them. As at Falkirk, even though it was now spring, with the yellow gorse starting to bloom, there was a cold and heavy rain, though, this time, the wind was not blowing it into the faces of the English.

Dismissing the suggestion that his men should have a meal before the battle, the duke commented: 'No. They'll fight all the better on empty bellies. Remember what a dessert they got to their dinner at Falkirk.' Addressing his troops as he rode through the lines, he said: 'My brave boys, your toil will soon be at an end. Stand your ground against the broadsword and target. Parry the enemy in the manner you have been directed...'[11]

Bonnie Prince Charlie had no more than 5,000 men, though the number gradually increased as other Highlanders arrived. Their weapons, in addition to the target or a larger shield, were muskets, pistols, dirks (short daggers) and claymores (double-edged broadswords). The weapons of the King's foot soldiers were mainly the kind of musket known as 'Brown Bess', with a 46in barrel and a weight of over 11lb, a detested burden on those long marches across Scotland. Each man's pouch was filled with twenty-four rounds of ammunition – that is, paper cartridges containing a ball or bullet and gunpowder.[12] This was superior to the Jacobite musketry, as was also the King's cavalry, its dragoons expert with sword, pistol and carbine. Finally the greatest advantage of the Royal Army was its artillery – sixteen 3-pounder cannon, with a range of 500 yards, as well as mortars.[13] The King's army also had superior numbers – 6,400 foot and 2,400 horse, one of the most formidable forces ever assembled in Britain.[14]

It was the artillery that opened the battle shortly after one o'clock. First, the Highlanders fired a few shots from their inferior batteries in an attempt to kill tlhe Duke of Cumberland, whose bulky figure on his big horse could be seen on the left flank. In reply Cumberland ordered a tremendous cannonade from his sixteen 3-pounders. Neither at Prestonpans nor at Falkirk had the Highlanders experienced any effective artillery fire, but now their ranks were seriously disrupted by this furious bombardment lasting almost half an hour, with more of the Prince's men lost in this opening cannonade than in the whole of the rest of the battle. The bloody damage was done not by individual cannon-balls, but by firing round iron-shot cannisters filled with shrapnel and finally grape-shot.[15]

Cumberland held back the infantry and allowed the artillery to complete its lethal work. However, noting that the Macdonalds were outflanking him over to his right, he brought up Puteney's Regiment, with the Yorkshire Blues, to the extreme right of the front line. At 1.30 p.m. the Highlanders, furiously impatient to get at the cannon and stop the murderous bombardment, started to advance on their right, soon to be blinded and confused by the dense clouds of smoke from the English gunpowder. Whenever the smoke cleared they could see the front rank of the redcoats kneeling to fire at them, then firing from the second and third rank standing behind them, providing a continuous hail of bullets.

In some places the Highlanders were too close to their enemies to use their muskets and pistols, so they hit out with their broadswords, crashing into the fixed bayonets, mainly of the regiments of Barell and Munro, on the English left flank. Over on the English right flank Pulteney's and the Blues, together with the Royal Scots, faced three courageous Highland charges by the Macdonalds, but cut them down with withering musket fire before they could reach the King's lines. The firing was so continuous, the duke later remarked, that 'the Royals and the Pulteney's hardly took their firelocks from their shoulders.'[16]

The battle now entered a phase of utter confusion, with blood-curdling cries and screams wherever the two sides became locked in hand-to-hand fighting, and with blade or bullet men were wounded, mutilated or slaughtered. At about 1.50 the Rebel army began to retreat, harrassed from the sides by constant firing, and by cavalry charges, especially those by Colonel Hawley's dragoons, who rode round the right flank of the rebels to attack them from the rear. On the English right, it was largely a matter of the dragoons finishing off the retreating Highlanders, their merciless onslaught being described in the account given by Blind Jack in one laconic sentence:

> Kingston's Light Horse pursued them in their disorder and flight, and made great slaughter amongst them.[17]

The mopping-up, to use the euphemistic military term, was the most brutal aspect of the Battle of Culloden, and did no credit to the English.

The man mainly responsible for the systematic killing of the wounded rebels left behind in the retreat was General Hawley. His orders were so uncompromising, giving no quarter to men who lay helpless on the battlefield, that he gained the well-deserved nickname of 'Hangman Hawley'. There is an interesting story that when he came upon one wounded

The site of Culloden.

Highland officer, the chief of the Fraser Clan, and ordered one of his own young officers to 'pistol the Rebel dog', he refused, and Hawley had to order somebody else to do the job. This compassionate officer who disobeyed orders was Major James Wolfe, with Barrell's Regiment, only nineteen at the time.[18] He had made an important contribution to the battle by the accurate musket fire of his men as they shot from behind an enclosure on the right of the charging Highlanders, breaking up their attack. He later became the famous General Wolfe, who thirteen years later would lose his life at the capture of Quebec.

Hawley's brutality towards the wounded was, alas, nothing compared with the atrocities which were to follow – and over a wide area of Scotland – all directed by the Duke of Cumberland, determined to stamp out the smouldering fire of the Rebellion once and for all. His own army was said to have lost no more than fifty killed and 259 wounded. The Jacobites, on the other hand, were said to have lost around 2,000 men, with hundreds more, including some supporting French troops, taken to Inverness as prisoners.[19] To this number there was now to be added the fleeing rebels whom the Redcoats were able to hunt down and subject to plunder, pillage, burnings and indiscriminate killings. All this was to some extend partly motivated by the frustration at not being able to find Bonnie Prince Charlie, who had escaped from the battlefield to ride off to the Outer Hebrides.

In Inverness the bells rang out to proclaim a great victory for King George, and in England and in the Scottish Lowlands, the Duke of Cumberland was hailed as a hero. Not so by many Scots, however, who saw Culloden not so much as a battle but as a massacre. When it was realised how ruthlessly Duke William Augustus was exterminating every trace of dissent, his nickname changed from 'Sweet William' to 'Stinking Billy', and his name would live on as the infamous 'Butcher Cumberland'.

John Metcalf relates none of this, not even an incident that he must have known about. Cumberland, as part of his policy to seek out civilian supporters of the rebels, ordered Colonel Cockayne, commander of Pulteney's, to take 200 volunteers (and these could have included some of the Yorkshire Blues) to go to Moy House, the home of the Laird of Mackintosh. On the way they looted and vandalised, and finally burst into the chieften's home, arresting the beautiful Lady Anne Moy, who was said to have raised the Clans, collectively known as the Clan Chatten, and even to have led them into battle at Culloden.[20]

The absence of Blind Jack's account of any reference to this, or the horrible aftermath of Culloden, could be explained by his unwillingness to record anything that was to the Duke of Cumberland's discredit. He had, after all, been on good terms with the son of King George, and – as he later admitted – he regretted that he had not seized the opportunity of making the most of this, because 'had he followed him to London, he would have received more marks of his royal favour'.[21]

What preoccupied Metcalf, of course, was getting back to Knaresborough – along with the rest of the Yorkshire Blues. Those who had been taken prisoner at Falkirk were now liberated and back with the rest of the company – all except two, Jack notes, who had died during captivity.[22] It must have been a glorious feeling as they set off in the warm air of spring, led by their musician, and with Captain Thornton riding beside them, on the long march from Scotland to Knaresborough.

The news of the victory of Culloden was greeted with jubilation throughout England. It was without doubt a milestone in British history. The King had been the last English monarch to lead his troops into battle, and now his son had decisively won what was to be the last battle to be fought on British soil. There was already talk of a thanksgiving service in St Paul's Cathedral, for which Handel would compose the popular chorus, later used in 'Judas Maccabaeus', but originally written in honour of the Duke of Cumberland:

See, the conquering hero comes!
Sound the trumpet! Beat the drums![23]

Many of his officers were also celebrated. In Knaresborough the feeling of pride is clearly shown by the way the people of the town felt they should honour Captain Thornton in some practical way. They were, said Hargrove, moved by the fact that because of his 'steady attachment to the rights and liberties of England', he had raised a company of soldiers, and 'marching at their head against the rebels into the mountains of Scotland' earned for himself 'the thanks, applause and esteem of every well-wisher to the constitution'.[24] So Knaresborough presented to Captain Thornton a token of esteem paid for by public donation – a small silver table, 2ft in diameter, which bore the following grandiose inscription:

Gulielmo Thornton, Arm.
Qui cum Cohorte Militum
Sumptu suo non mediocri

Sustentata
Pro Rege et Patria
In Scotia contra Rebelles
Improbissima Hyeme
Belli periculis
Sese magnanimiter
Obtulit
Anno Dom. MDCCXLV (1745)

(To William Thornton, Knight at Arms, who with a Company of Soldiers, maintained at his own not inconsiderable expense, for King and Country, in Scotland, in the most inclement winter, magnanimously offered himself to confront the dangers of war. In the Year of our Lord 1745.)[25]

This Latin inscription was on the upper side of the table, and was repeated on the underside, with the addition of the words (following the date) of *Burgus Knaresburgensis*, and (following *Hyeme*) of *Relicta Conjuge*, referring to the wife he left behind. As the word 'relict' is also used to mean 'widow', it is interesting to see that Hargrove makes it clear that Thornton's wife was very much alive, by relating the following anecdote – one that Blind Jack must surely have known. Soon after Culloden, Captain Thornton and his lady were invited to court, no doubt at the duke's suggestion. George II, apparently struck by the beauty of Mrs Thornton, addressed the captain as follows:

Mr Thornton, I have been told of the services you have rendered to your country, and your attachment to me and my family, and have held myself obliged to you for both; but I was never able to estimate the degree of the obligation till now, that I see the lady whom you left behind you.[26]

William Thornton certainly did well out of his venture with the Knaresborough-recruited soldiers. As a Member of Parliament he went on to work with the support of General Oglethorpe to establish a permanent militia, building on his own success with the Yorkshire Blues. He published his views in 1752, and in 1759, the year he sent Eugene Aram for trial, he was promoted to colonel and appointed commandant of the first Regiment of Militia in Yorkshire, later that year becoming MP for York a second time.[27] Thornton, acknowledged as the first important champion of the militia in England, always claimed that if it had existed properly in 1745 the country would have saved £3 million because no enemy would have thought of invading it.[28] Thornton certainly never forgot his indebtedness to Blind Jack in helping to set up and lead his pioneer militia of Yorkshire Blues, and remained a good friend for the rest of his life.

What of the rank and file following Culloden? Were they shown the same appreciation as their officers? We can assume that they were, even if it is unrecorded. Just a glimpse of the general rejoicing in Knaresborough can be seen in a record showing that the churchwardens paid seven shillings to the bell ringers for celebrating 'the defeat of the rebels at Culloden.'[29]

We can picture the general delight in Knaresborough and the surrounding villages at the safe return of the menfolk, particularly the joy of Dolly Metcalf, as she welcomed home 'her poor blind adventurer', as she called him. Jack did not want any medals or presentations. Sufficient for him that, 'He had the happiness to find his faithful partner and children in good health', records the editor, and adds that although Dolly had often been afraid for him, 'knowing that a spirit of enterprise made part of his nature', she was often comforted by the hope that he would 'in some degree signalize himself, notwithstanding the misfortune under which he laboured'. Though we can be sure that neither of the two expressed themselves in this kind of literary language, we can imagine the old man recalling their rapturous reunion, reflected in the written paraphrase:

This declaration, following a most cordial reception, gave full conformation to an opinion which Metcalf had ever held, viz. that the caresses and approbation of the softer sex are the highest reward a soldier can deserve or obtain.[30]

There was a very special pleasure reserved for his homecoming. Dolly had recently given birth to their fourth child, baptised on 20 March 1746, and named John, after his father.[31] Now, it seemed, Blind Jack would settle down and stay at home as a good family man. But it was not to be for long.

Chapter Ten

Trader, Smuggler, Wagoner: The First Road

We do not know the exact date when Blind Jack arrived back in Knaresborough from Scotland, but it was probably in late April or early May, and an ideal time for him to resume his work as a spa musician, based at the Queen's Head, for the beginning of the new season.

Now that there was a new baby in the house, as well as three older children to feed and clothe, he needed the steady income provided by his music making. He would also have his accumulated army pay. By the time the Yorkshire Blues were disbanded and he had returned to civilian life, this must have amounted (at the shilling a day previously mentioned) to nearly £8 for the five months of service – perhaps a good deal more in the case of a musician, who would be paid above the rank of a private. We know, for example, that Thornton's sergeants and drummers received '1s 2d per diem'.[1] But he still needed more money, and soon found it in several business ventures.

Always ready to form friendships, especially if he thought there was any financial advantage in it, he had used his time in Aberdeen to make both enquiries and contacts. He had become very interested in the clothing produced in Scotland, mainly worsteds and cotton, including the well-known Aberdeen stockings. So Dolly had to say farewell to him a second time. He set off for Scotland, renewed his earlier contacts, and procured a great quantity of cloth and clothing, which he brought back to set himself up in business in England. He sold these items, not at local markets, but by going round to the country houses where he had played at dances, and where he found a ready sale, and made a good profit. Dolly presumably kept his accounts, but he claimed that 'amongst a thousand articles' he always knew what each had cost him, because of a specially made price tag that he could feel.[2]

Such was the abounding energy of this well-built, exceptionally fit man, still only in his early thirties, that he added to his trade in clothing from Scotland a trade in horses. He had already done this on a small scale in Yorkshire, but now he became a recognised horse-dealer, taking horses up to Scotland and exchanging them for the smaller horses known as 'galloways'. So named because they were originally bred in Galloway (like the small black hornless cattle, also called galloways), they were a kind of pony of no more than fifteen hands. Galloways became so popular in Yorkshire, where they were well suited to work in the Dales, that gallowa became a standard term in Yorkshire dialect for a small horse.[3]

Journeys to Scotland, and mixing with all kinds of traders and dealers, brought Blind Jack into contact with smugglers. He already had a reputation for sharp dealing – what was generally known as 'the Yorkshire bite' – and now he was tempted to gain extra money by breaking the law, his admission of this being summed up in the brief understatement:

> He also engaged pretty deeply in the contraband trade, the profits of which were at the time much more considerable than the risk.[4]

Not all the details of his smuggling activities are disclosed, but he dictated a few stories of this life, no doubt proud that he had not been caught, and also enjoying the opportunity to boast about his remarkable cunning and indomitable persistence. On one occasion, he claims, in response to an urgent summons, he rode out from Knaresborough at three in the morning and got to Newcastle by six o'clock in the evening – 'a distance of nearly

74 miles, and did not feel the least fatigued'. Here he received some contraband packages, and managed to get them conveyed to a wagon by a few soldiers, these being the least likely to come under suspicion. Having dispatched the smuggled goods, he packed a hundredweight of untaxed tea into a huge saddle bag, where it was concealed beneath tow and rough flax. When he passed the office of an excise man at Chester-le-Street, he told the officer that his huge package was tow for his aunt, who lived just a few miles away – feasible enough, as it was known that Jack had relatives in the area. He got the tea back to Knaresborough, and sold it at a good profit.

This was a time when there were complaints in Parliament about the high price of tea, and it was estimated that half the tea drunk in England was smuggled through the customs. So Jack's illicit trade was typical of the period, and he does not seem to have regarded it as a truly criminal activity. It was simply part of the well-organised black market trade that he had met on the east coast of Scotland, and he even earns an honoured mention in the annals of Scottish trafficking.[5]

The smuggling was so profitable that he sometimes invested in it by transferring money from what he made as a horse-dealer. On one occasion he sold a whole string of horses and used £200 of the profit to buy a large quantity of rum, brandy and tea – much of it contraband. He arranged to have it sent by ship to Leith, the port of Edinburgh, where he waited for its arrival. After six weeks with no news, he was in such 'distress of mind' at the prospect of losing all his investment that he remembers he wished he had been lost at sea – as he assumed the ship to have been. But the vessel arrived soon afterwards, and he boarded her, intending to complete the journey to Newcastle, where he had family and friends. However, his thoughts of being lost at sea now came close to being realised. A great storm arose, washing the ship's mate overboard, carrying away the mainsail, and driving the ship towards the rocky coast of Norway. Jack – who had some experience of sailing in coastal vessels – was convinced that they would sink, and all on board be drowned:

> It now appeared a dreadful thing to leave the world in the midst of health and vigour; but the wind changing, hope began to return, and the captain put about for the Scotch coast, intending to make Arbroath. A signal of distress was put up, but the sea ran so high that no boat could venture out with a pilot.[6]

The captain managed to steer the ship towards the harbour, but she struck the pier, before being towed round into a safe berth. A group of locals had gathered in the expectation of plundering a vessel they took to be a virtual wreck, but were driven away by an officer and twenty men from Pulteney's Regiment, who recognised Jack from serving with him in Scotland. Ironically, they were there in pursuit of smugglers, but were happy to provide a guard for Jack and the crew as they moved cargo from the flooded ship into a warehouse.

Jack later transferred his own £200 worth of goods to another ship, on which he sailed safely down to Newcastle. Here he struck a deal with a man he thought he could trust. He told him that on board the ship he had 400 gallons of gin and brandy, for which he had a customs permit, and thirty for which had none. A quarter of an hour later all his goods were seized and brought ashore, this man having betrayed him to the excise men. With his customary cunning and network of acquaintances he eventually managed to get it all back – through conversations with Mr Sunderland, the collector, and a letter from Alderman Pereth, both of whom he knew.[7]

In an 1811 edition of Metcalf's memoirs, printed in Knaresborough by Hargrove & Sons, a footnote is added at this point describing an incident which happened when he was riding on the road near Darlington, on his way back to Knaresborough. A voice he knew asked him where he had come from. His answer is worth quoting as evidence of his casual attitude to smuggling:

> I have been in Scotland, where I was before, with Colonel Thornton, at Falkirk races. But now I have been drinking whiskey amongst the redshanks, and doing a little business in the smuggling line – but, pray, how does all friends at Knaresborough?' Surprised at the question the person replied, 'Why, Jack, do you not know me?' After a short pause Jack replied, 'It is Mr Thomas Cass, the glazier, of Knaresborough.'[8]

Back in Knaresborough a new opportunity presented itself – this one helping him to move more decisively in the direction of road building. A regiment called the Queen's Bays had been raised, and was quartered in Knaresborough and other neighbouring towns. When they were ordered to move north there was a need for baggage transport, for which local wagons were not readily supplied, the army paying only ninepence a mile per ton. Blind Jack decided to offer his two big wagons, each drawn by four horses. They were loaded, and riding on his own horse, he accompanied them all the way to Durham. There he met another regiment needing transport – Bland's Dragoons, who had been at Culloden. As they were moving down to York, he agreed to carry their baggage as far as Northallerton. The journey from Knaresborough and back took him six days, for which he made a profit of £20.[9]

As soon as he heard that the Queen's Bays were having new horses provided, and that some of the existing ones were being sold off, he rode up to Durham through the night, to make sure he did not miss the sale. With his usual tactics he made discreet enquiries, gathering half-a-dozen of the army farriers together, plying them with plenty of gin, and getting them to tell him which were the best horses. He discovered that one of these was a fine grey horse belonging to the drummers. However, through carelessness in trimming its coat, ready for the sale, this poor stallion had been caught on the penis, which was now grossly swollen. At the sale Blind Jack first bought a bay horse, ideal for pulling a carriage:

> They then brought forward the grey horse with his swelled sheath, which excited many jokes and much laughter among the spectators. Our chapman [Blind Jack] bought him also, at the very low price of £3. 15.s, which was first affixed by the auctioneer, but which, however, the people said was very much beyond his value.[10]

Blind Jack got his genitally swollen horse back to Knaresborough, looked after him like the experienced horseman he was, and soon found he was back to normal. He was offered fifteen guineas for him, but kept him for many years as a draught horse. In fact, Jack was so enjoying his work as a horse-and-cart man that he decided to take it to its logical conclusion and set up a regular wagon service between York and Knaresborough. He did the driving himself, once a week in winter and twice a week in summer, fitting his journeys in between his continuing sessions at the spa. He started his stage-wagon business – the first of its kind between York and Knaresborough – in 1751, when he was still only thirty-four. His wagon-service, which also included the conveyance of passengers too poor to afford a stagecoach, lasted a couple of years, during which time he completed his apprenticeship in coping with English roads and all their deficiences. There could not have been a fitter prelude or better preparation for the new career which now followed, when he moved from regularly using roads, to actually making them.

This was an interesting period in the development of road building in Britain. We have already seen (Chapter 5) that travel, and as a consequence, the economy, was greatly impeded by the state of the roads. Their unsatisfactory nature was mainly the result of ordinary parishioners being expected to keep them in good repair, and occasionally being brought before the Quarter Sessions when they failed to do this as can be seen in Yorkshire records.[11]

There is no lack of evidence of difficult communications in Blind Jack's part of Yorkshire – and not just on the long journeys he had made to London and Scotland. In the early years of the eighteenth century the road from Leeds to York, for example, was so bad that diarists like Ralph Thoresby recorded how this main road was in places 'dangerous for a coach' and they had to get out and walk.[12] As the century unfolded, there was a gradual improvement, even though many still deplored, as in Fielding's *Tom Jones* (1749), 'the very execrable roads'. Throughout the country turnpike trusts were being set up, mainly by landowners, to repair and renew stretches of road, controlling them by means of turnpike toll gates and toll houses.

Each turnpike was controlled by trustees or commissioners appointed by the particular Turnpike Act, with the day-to-day running of the Turnpikes administered by three officers – the surveyor, the clerk and the treasurer.[13] By the end of 1750 there were 146 turnpike trusts. Yet between 1750 and 1772 no fewer than 418 new trusts were formed, making the total distance covered by turnpike roads more than 15,000 miles.[14] Blind Jack's work was part of this rapid expansion of new highways.

His opportunity came while he was still doing well with his stage-wagon business – which he immediately sold to a man called Guiseley. He does not give us the actual date when he started on his new career, and some writers have guessed it as 1765, which is far too late.[15] It was, in fact, in 1752, when a new Turnpike Act (officially designated 25 Geo.IIc 58) was passed, authorising the repairing, widening and rebuilding of the road between Harrogate and Boroughbridge. The account book of the 'Harrogate to Boroughbridge Turnpike Trust (1752-1870)' records that on 15 November 1752 it appointed Thomas Oastler as its surveyor. Already appointed clerk to the Trust, in fact, he now took on overall responsibility:

> The said Thomas Oastler hath offered and proposed himself for Treasurer and Surveyor of the said Road… and is likewise elected Unanimously.[16]

This was the man who was to launch Blind Jack on his road-building career.

Oastler, who lived in the village of Farnham, 2 miles north of Knaresborough, was looking for somebody to whom he could contract the work. It is possible that he knew Metcalf through a mutual friend, William Woodburn, who is mentioned as a fellow executor in a Knaresborough will.[17] Perhaps it was over a drink in one of the local pubs that Blind Jack, 'falling into company with him', as Metcalf put it, talked himself into being given the job, and agreed to make about 3 miles of the road between the villages of Minskip and Ferrensby (the amanuensis misheard this as 'Fearnsby'). It seems incredible that the thirty-five-year-old Metcalf should have been given such a contract at all. The question must be asked: how on earth could a blind man build roads?

The answer is that Blind Jack did not do this work single-handed. He organised and motivated others to build roads for him. Above all things, he was – as Thomas Oastler must have known – a born leader of men, respected for his energetic drive and good humour, his quick thinking, his practical knowledge of both horses and men, his military experience, his wide experience of life, and the way he had mastered its frustations and obstacles.

Above: Toll-house, North Deighton.

Left: A turnpike boundary stone, Harrogate.

His first task was to recruit good workmen – just as he had recruited good men for the Yorkshire Blues only seven years earlier – and, indeed, some of those former soldiers would now make up his workforce.

From the outset it must be acknowledged that Blind Jack's achievement in making roads was entirely dependent on numerous gangs of anonymous men who did the donkey work. In the neatly kept Turnpike Trust account book, which gives details of expenditure for his first road, it is interesting to see how frequently the actual workmen are mentioned. For example:

Nov. 3	To labourers on the road	£4.8.6.
10.	To labourers on the road	£7.6.11.
17.	To labourers on the road	£7.3.0.[18]

Having given due credit to the manual labourers who did the actual job, toiling away in all kinds of weather with pick, spade and shovel, it is important to point out that Blind Jack did not simply stand there organising the road building by shouting out orders from the sideline. From the beginning he was involved in every aspect of the work, as eyewitnesses testify, quite literally hands on, as he prodded with his stick, felt for himself the state of the ground, checked the depth of the digging, and the stone and gravel they were using to make the road. The general course of the road would usually already exist, with modifications and additions specified by the surveyor. But it would require radical digging out in most places, and much draining and levelling.

For his Minskip-Ferrensby road he managed to find a single gravel pit big enough to supply the whole length of 3 miles. Here he based the men who would dig up the gravel and load it onto wagons, and for them he built a temporary shelter out of deal boards, and 'racks and mangers' for a dozen horses. Three-quarters of a mile away, at Minskip, he hired a house for the men who would lay down the stones and gravel.

Yorkshire road-makers in Blind Jack's day. (G. Walker, *Costumes of Yorkshire*, 1814)

He made sure that his men worked hard, starting each day as early as possible, and also saw to it that they were well fed. The personal example he set them is illustrated by his account of how he often walked the 2 miles from Knaresborough before any of them had started work, carrying four or five stone of meat on his shoulders, and joining his men by six o'clock.[19]

We shall examine Blind Jack's techniques of road building in the next chapter, but it should be said at this point that behind all the practical work of measuring distances and estimating quantities there was a remarkably acute mind. All kinds of little instances show that Metcalf was a good mathematician and had a real flair for quantity surveying. One of his methods was to put his arms round a piece of timber, for example, and calculate from its girth and length what it would be in square feet and inches. Even in his last years he was using this trick to gauge the quantity of hay in a stack.[20]

Jack seems to have prided himself on his ability to give an accurate estimate of bulk. According to one Victorian antiquary there was a strong tradition that he used to visit the gigantic Cowthorpe Oak, situated about 5 miles to the south-east of Knaresborough. This tree, which I saw in the 1950s, when it was reduced to a mere stump, was in Blind Jack's day reputed to be the biggest and oldest in England – over 40ft high, 60ft in circumference, and over 1,000 old. Jack liked to use his arms to work out the girth of the tree at various heights, pointing accurately with his stick to where a massive branch had been broken off in 1710. He came so frequently to feel his way round this tree that it was said that whenever he came, an old bloodhound, which was kept nearby, and which used to snarl at every stranger, fondled him and licked his hand – another instance of Jack's affinity with animals.[21]

The Cowthorpe Oak, incidentally, provided Blind Jack with one of his two surviving sticks, cut from a branch. This is the stout stick, once kept in Knaresborough Castle, now to be seen with his effigy in the Knaresborough Courthouse Museum. This stick was originally 5ft 3in in length, the last 27in having been accidentally broken off in 1870 by the wife of the castle caretaker, who took it on a nutting expedition to Birkham Woods.[22] Whereas this heavy-duty staff was what Blind Jack would use for prodding and poking during his road-making, the more slender cherry-wood stick (seen in the 1795 portrait, and now displayed at Knaresborough House; a photograph of this stick can be seen on page 85) would be used essentially for feeling his way.

Though Metcalf clearly had no problem with mental arithmetic, and could apparently reel off figures measurement and precise sums of money, all remembered with ease, it is obvious that he must have had help in keeping accounts, and we can assume that this was readily provided by Dolly, who had been his treasurer in the days before their marriage. It would now have been a great satisfaction to her to see the family income now start to grow. Once Blind Jack started on this lucrative career of road building, he would have an earning capacity far above what he had been able to make as a musician, supplemented by his various business ventures.

The 3 miles of road which Oastler employed Blind Jack to build were part of the gently winding, slightly undulating stretch leading from Knaresborough north-east to Boroughbridge. It formed an important link between two old market towns, and also gave access to the Great North Road. The work presented no special difficulties, and it would have given Jack the chance to show what he could do. If he made a good job of this, he and his team could be given further commissions. We do not know how long it took, but it is recorded that 'he completed the work much sooner than expected, to the entire satisfaction of the surveyor and the trustees'.[23] This must be set in the context of the general standard of turnpike roads, some of which, as we have seen, were described by contemporary users as very unsatisfactory.

There is a special pleasure in riding, and especially walking, on this road today, now the A6055. The views are picturesque and peaceful, and there is the thought that only a matter of inches below the modern metalled surface is the old road laid down by Blind Jack and his men in 1752. It was his boast that his roads would need no repair for at least a dozen years. So this was by no means one of his extravagant claims.

I have had the privilege of taking people over Blind Jack's first road when programmes have been made for the media. The first was for BBC's Radio Four series for the blind, *In Touch*, in 1995. The second, also for Radio Four, was in 2001, when a programme was made by Gary O'Donoghue, who had been blind from the age of eight. It was fascinating to see Gary handling the actual stick – the cherry-wood stick seen in the portrait – that Blind Jack used. I remember how he held this under his right forearm as he reconstructed the way Jack would have held it, this being confirmed, Gary said, by the side the tip showed most wear. This stick, nearly 7ft in length, was not, of course, used as a walking stick, but as what is now called a 'long cane', used with a sweeping motion to detect obstacles.

Gary was particularly interested in the viameter that Metcalf had had specially made for his accurate measurement of the roads. This is essentially a wooden wheel, with wooden spokes and an iron-clad rim, nearly 3ft in diameter. From each side of the hub a straight piece of wood, concealing the mechanism, goes up to a sturdy wooden handle, on which there is a circular brass dial with a pointer. The dial has calibrations, incised on the metal, so that Blind Jack could feel the exact distance, in feet and furlongs, that he had pushed his viameter. Also called a waywiser or odometer, a smaller and lighter version of this measuring device, working on exactly the same principle, is still used by modern surveyors.

The original viameter, pushed over his roads by Blind Jack, can be seen in Knaresborough's Courthouse Museum. I have been allowed to handle it and take it outside for the purpose of a photograph, and we used it briefly, pushing it along the very first Metcalf road in a feature on Blind Jack in the 'Great Lives' series on BBC Television's *Look North* in 1997. It is so valuable, however, that I had to have a near-replica of it made when I included Blind Jack in my presentation of the Knaresborough Millennium Pageant in 2000,[24] and it was trundled through the streets of the town. (Another viameter, incidentally, less substantial, said to have belonged to Blind Jack, used to be exhibited at the Wakeman's House, Ripon.)

Gary O'Donoghue's comments, while he was identifying with his blind predecessor, of similar bulk to himself, really were of historical value. One of the reasons Jack was able to get around so easily, he said, was that his horse, with whom he had such a close bond, acted as a kind of guide dog – sometimes with better effect, because horses can show more sensitivity and reliability than dogs. When he came to work on roads he would have far more awareness of the ground under his feet than a sighted person. As a blind person, he told me, you are bound to be acutely aware of every obstacle and pot hole, and habitually listen to the sound of your footsteps.

Those who drive between Knaresborough and Boroughbridge today on this comparatively quiet rural road are, with very few exceptions, unaware that they are travelling over historic ground. This was to be the first of an estimated 180 miles of road that Blind Jack of Knaresborough would build in Yorkshire and in four other counties. The original surface of locally quarried gravel, hidden beneath the modern tarmac, was to be the foundation of his fame.

The author demonstrating the use of Blind Jack's viameter. (Courtesy of the Knaresborough Court House Museum)

Chapter Eleven

Pioneer Road Builder

Before we look at the methods Blind Jack used in his new career of road building and give an account of his extensive network of highways, we must note – with some surprise, perhaps – that his next project, after that first Minskip-Ferrensby contract, was to build not a road, but a bridge. This was to be one of many bridges that he would build as a kind of adjunct to his main work.

Shortly before his first road was completed he heard that tenders were being put out for the building of a new bridge over the little River Tut, which flows through the centre of Boroughbridge to join the Ure (not to be confused, as some writers have done, with the very much larger bridge over the river Ure, or the other smaller bridge in St Helen Street).[1] Jack went along to discuss this at the Crown inn, Boroughbridge, no doubt encouraged to do so by Thomas Oastler, who had, in addition to his turnpike position, been appointed as surveyor for the new bridge, and now presided over this meeting of local gentlemen and stonemasons. The estimates they had before them varied considerably, so Oastler told the meeting that, although John Metcalf had not built a bridge before, the tender he could offer was worthy of being considered. Jack was invited to appear before the committee and put his case. He was first asked what, if anything, he knew about bridges. His response was to give specific measurements of his proposed Tut Bridge, already worked out by examining the river and making calculations. Asking them to draw a rough plan and write down his figures, he concisely gave his specifications:

> The span of the arch, 18 feet, being a semi-circle, makes 27: the arch-stones must be a foot deep, which if multiplied by 27, will be 386; and the bases will be 72 feet more. This for the arch: it will require good backing; for which purpose there are proper stones in the old Roman wall at Aldborough, which may be brought, if you please to give directions to that effect.[2]

The gentlemen of the committee were all impressed by Metcalf's straightforward, practical approach. With the confirmation of their chairman's assurance that he had made an excellent job of his road, they agreed to give him the contract.

His philistine suggestion that they could use suitable stones from a nearby Roman wall might have raised eyebrows. Even in those pre-conservationist days there would have been some awareness that Alborough was a priceless archaeological site, bearing remains of the 60-acre walled city of Isurium Brigantum, the most northerly of the Romano-British settlements. This is probably why they decided the stones should be purchased from the quarry of a man called Renton, one of the masons who had put in a tender. However, along with the other masons who resented the contract going to an amateur like Metcalf, this Renton was 'much offended', and refused to sell any of his stone for the building of the bridge. Jack solved this by going to the lime-kilns at Farnham, not far from his nearly-finished road. There he found lots of good stone which the lime-burners had discarded. He arranged to have it dressed and made into suitable blocks for building, then got his men to convey these to Boroughbridge.

As soon as he had completed his road contract, Blind Jack started work on the Tut Bridge and claimed that he 'completed the arch in one day, and the whole in a very short period'.[3] This is difficult to believe, yet we cannot simply dismiss Blind Jack's claims as fanciful exaggerations. The span of the arch, measured today, is exactly 18ft – the figure he gave, and later quoted from memory, after a lapse of forty-two years! The other measurements fit his description of what he intended to build, with the top of the semi-circular arch 8ft above the riverbed, and a width of 40ft, with a slight change in direction halfway, following the course of the river.[4]

In the *Look North* television programme previously referred to, I was able to show viewers what a fine little bridge this is. Though once repaired after a flood, it is essentially as Blind Jack built it in early 1753. As the full view is only accessible from a private garden, people who walk or drive along Fishergate towards Boroughbridge Market Place are usually unaware that they are passing over a small river. But underneath the street is one of the few constructions made by Blind Jack that we can actually see. Unlike his roads, concealed beneath our modern surfaces, we have visible and tangible evidence in this much-used bridge that has survived more than two and a half centuries.

Soon after he had completed Tut Bridge Thomas Oastler, who was pleased both with this and the Minskip-Ferrensby road, offered Metcalf a contract to build a mile and a half of the important road from the Knaresborough's High Bridge, leading up the hill and across to Harrogate. The existing poor road went up to join Bilton Lane, veering to the right. This new turnpike would take a direct route to High Harrogate, passing through the village of Starbeck, which a hundred years later would become an important railway centre.

It appears that Blind Jack started his stretch of road from the Starbeck end, and one of his first jobs was the construction of another small bridge, so his road could be carried over the Star Beck. This stream still flows, but there is nothing left of the bridge, incorporated into later roadworks.

How did Blind Jack build his roads? In the first place, he did not rely on reports given to him by the surveyor, he liked to do his own surveying, feeling the ground by walking over it, prodding it with his stick and measuring it with his viameter. Having surveyed the terrain and confirmed the route, Blind Jack would then order his men to stake out any new stretches, remove the turf and large stones, occasionally – as the records show – blasting rock away with gunpowder. They would then dig out the soil to a depth of as much as 18in (McAdam's roads, considerably later, tended to be only around 10in deep).[5] Less clearance and digging would, of course, be needed whenever he used an existing road, but the depth of both new stretches and repaired sections would be roughly the same, the aim being to make sure that the final road had a sound foundation and allowed a smooth passage over it.

He seems to have paid particular attention to making a level surface, free from holes and declivities. One of his workmen recalled how he used to walk over the road, feeling with his feet and prodding away with his stick. Then, whenever he found a hollow place, he would call out in his usual dialect: 'Ere! Let's 'a' some in 'ere!'[6]

The standard procedure was to fill in the excavated road with three kinds of material: first a layer of fairly large pieces of stone, then one of smaller stones (no bigger than 'a hen's egg', in the case of McAdam), and finally a layer of gravel that would eventually be bedded down by the pressure of hooves and wheels into a reasonably smooth surface. There are many references in the Turnpike Trust's accounts to payment for 'gravel', and for the small round stones beneath this, usually described as 'cobbles' (such as 'to cobbles gathering at Minskip, £18.5.ll.').[7]

GRAVEL

MIDDLE STONES

STRONG STONES

BUNDLES OF HEATHER

AND GORSE ROOTS

20 FEET WIDE

EIGHTEEN INCHES

SIXTEEN INCHES

DRAIN

Above: A cross-section of Blind Jack's road design.

Left: Blind Jack's first road: Minskip–Ferrensby (1752).

Opposite above: Blind Jack's first roads (marked in as dark lines) as shown in the Hargrove's map of 1795.

Opposite below: Tut Bridge (built in 1753).

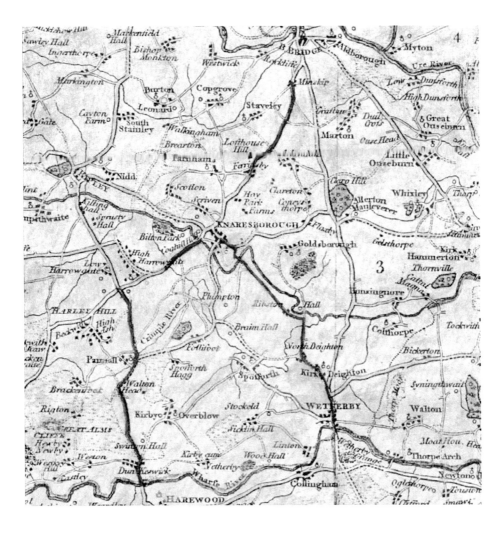

In the minute books of some Turnpike Trusts there is a specific record of the standard Blind Jack worked to. The road was usually stoned to a width of 20ft made in a converse shape, 18in deep in the middle, 16in at the sides. The lowest part was to be 8in of 'strong stone', then 6in of 'middle stone', and finally 4in of small broken hard stone or gravel.[8] (See diagram on the previous page.)

The tendency for roads to become soft and boggy, with water-filled hollows, was counteracted not just by the provision of a new surface, but by the digging out of drains along each side of the road. In connection with this there are interesting references in the accounts to the Knaresborough stonemason who was to prove an important witness in the trial of Eugene Aram, six years later (His borrowed mason's pick had allegedly been used for the murder). For example:

To William Tuton for getting stones and laying drains £0.17.6.[9]

This suggests that Blind Jack's drains, here at least, were not simply ditches, but lined with stone.

Most of this was largely the accepted way of making roads, successfully used by General Wade in rainy Scotland. What was original about Blind Jack's technique was that he devised a clever way of taking a road over badly waterlogged ground, which in many cases would have required the road to make a detour. His practice was to order great quantities of heather and gorse, pulled up by the roots, and have lengths of their tough and springy stems and roots tied into bundles. These he placed at the bottom of his excavation, making a layer of criss-crossed bundles. On top of this porous foundation he spread the usual layers of stones, and finally a layer of gravel. Unlikely as it may seem, this odd combination seems to have worked, eventually becoming compressed and consolidated into a dry and durable road.

This section of the Knaresborough-Harrogate road was mostly over dry ground, and one part was over a grassy area under which they found 'an old causeway, supposed to have been made in the time of the Romans'. Though he had been restrained from similar vandalism at Aldborough, he had no scruples here about having this broken up, and the material used for his road. As they moved towards High Bridge, however, they encountered the swampy ground which allowed him to try his first experiment of using what in Yorkshire dialect is known as whin (gorse or furze) and ling (heather).

Between the Forest Lane Head and Knaresborough Bridge, there was a bog, in a low piece of ground, over which to have passed was the nearest way; and the surveyor thought it impossible to make a road over it: but Metcalf assured him that he could readily accomplish it. The other then told him that if so he should be paid for the same length as if he had gone round. Jack set about it, cast the road up, and covered it with whin and ling; and made it as good or better than any part he had undertaken.[10]

Confirmation of the existence of this boggy area can be found in an adjacent field, part of which near the road has a tendency to become waterlogged. Also, within yards of the road is a spring (shown on large-scale Ordinance Survey maps), traditionally used by Blind Jack for his workmen.[11]

Blind Jack's use of whin or gorse, is confirmed in a surviving, almost illegible fragment of a bill, unfortunately with no date. The bill also refers to 'leading' (moving by cart) and to the other materials he used. After months of attempting to decipher this, I realised that one obscure word was kids, a dialect term for the bundles or fagots into which the gorse was already tied.

Mr John Metcalf	Dr to J.Crosby
2 days Leading	12. 0.
and Day	6. 6.
40 Whin Kids	1. 6.
Leading	1. 8.
Cart Load of Tree Tops	1. 0.
5 Threaves Straw	6. 0.
Lock and …(?)	10. 0.
Bringing wood from park	2. 6.
Peck of Oates	0. 7.
3 lagings of Straw	5. 0.
	£1 14s 6d[12]

For this Knaresborough-Harrogate road the surveyor ordered at least some of the stone himself. We also know from the account book of the 'Harrogate to Borrowbridge Turnpike Trust 1752-1870' that from quite an early stage Thomas Oastler was able almost to balance his expenses by income from tolls (e.g. 13 February 1752, 'Laid out upon the road, £668. 17. 10¼, Recd. by the road £656. 06. 09.') He would not have begrudged the total of 'about £400 for the road and a small bridge' which Blind Jack states he was paid.[13] This figure is more than confirmed by the account book, which shows he received it in instalments:

23 July 1753:	To John Metcalf in part	£80 5s ½d
13 December 1753:	To John Metcalf in part	£352 17s 0d
28 January 1754:	To John Metcalf in full	£118 1s 2d
10 August 1754:	To John Metcalf for High Bridge End	£17 14s 3d

This means that Blind Jack received a total of a little over £568, proving that he was giving a modest understatement of what he had earned.[14]

Jack had made such a good job of his first three small contracts that he was now able to expand his business, and tackle a piece of work that would bring him in far more money than he and Dolly could have dreamed possible. Moreover, they were already in a better financial position after the first turnpike payments, and Jack, unable to resist a little speculation, had just bought an old house with land in Harrogate for £8, then sold it three weeks later for more than £200.[15]

He secured his next contract by attending the meeting arranged by Henry Lascelles (later Lord Harewood), where he was awarded it in competition with 'a great number of estimates' attracted by this profitable contract. The trustees, having noted that John Metcalf had a recent record of good work, finished on or before time, and that he had an air of authority and general competence, decided that this was sufficient to outweigh the handicap of his blindness, and justified giving him the contract. This would have been much to the surprise and annoyance of his rivals, when they realised they had been beaten by a blind man offering a lower tender. It was a substantial undertaking – 4 miles between Harrogate and Harewood Bridge, part of a major road into Leeds.

The agreement was that it had to be completed before the start of the winter of 1754. In addition, because much of the ground was stiff clay Jack decided to 'cast' the road (i.e. dig it out) over the whole length, before he started laying down any of the stone. He therefore came to another agreement with the trustees that no carriages should be allowed to pass during their digging – unlike the case with the road between Knaresborough and Starbeck. To make sure that no carriage trespassed onto these roadworks, but took the longer detour, he had a sluice or ditch dug across each end, with easily-erected wooden bridges to allow his own carts and wagons to pass to and fro. As in his first job at Minskip, he rented two houses along the route to provide accommodation for workmen not travelling from home.

Once again, there was boggy ground for the road to cross, and he needed a bigger quantity than before of whin and ling roots. So he personally surpervised a team of nine horses pulling a wheel-plough, which he found an effective way of digging out the strong roots. The whole road of almost 6 miles was finished in the time allowed – and for this he received a sum he really was entitled to boast about – £1,200.[16] This single payment (though we do not know how much of the sum was actual profit) was more than he could have earned as a fiddler in several years, and from this time it is possible that he stopped his regular playing at Harrogate, though he still occasionally played for dances there, and especially at the country houses, where he was always welcome.

Metcalf's own account of his successful new career rarely includes any references to problems and setbacks. Yet there must have been many. This very road from Harrogate had angered locals by the imposition of new tolls. Not long before Blind Jack had started there was, in June 1753, a riot which threatened to put a stop to his work altogether. A huge mob, armed with weapons ranging from muskets to pitchforks, marched out from Leeds to destroy the turnpike that had been set up at Harewood Bridge. Having been warned that the mob was on its way, Edwin Lascelles quickly assembled a small army of 300 of his tenants and workmen. When the two sides clashed there was a furious battle in which two or three were killed, many injured, and thirty sent to prison.[17]

After this the roadworks were well guarded, and Blind Jack does not refer to any trouble – but he must have been aware of local hostility to certain aspects of his turnpike roads. Opposition came mainly from those who were expected to pay tolls when taking very short journeys from one village to another – or just going to the market.[18] In 1753 toll-bars and gates were attacked and burnt down in places like Otley, and James Taylor, a toll-bar keeper on the Halifax-Wakefield turnpike, was paid 40 shillings in compensation 'for damages which he suffered by the Rioters in or about 1753.'[19]

Nor can it always have been easy for him to control his men, who in the later stages of his road building amounted to several hundred. Some would be local men he had worked with before, or even served with in the army in Scotland. Others would be general labourers, sometimes working on the farms. The term 'navvies' or navigators, the rough, tough gangs, toiling away to dig out the course of canals and railways, was not used until the early nineteenth century, but Blind Jack's men were the forerunners of these.[20] Many were hard drinking, as well as hard working, a fact reflected in G.K. Chesterton's epigram:

The rolling English drunkard
Made the rolling English road.[21]

Blind Jack was an experienced hard-drinker himself, and would have understood such men. This may have been one reason why (with just one recorded exception – we shall later consider) he never seems to have had trouble with them. This is coupled with the fact that he seems to have been exceptionally well organised, always in control yet willing to work alongside his early day navvies.

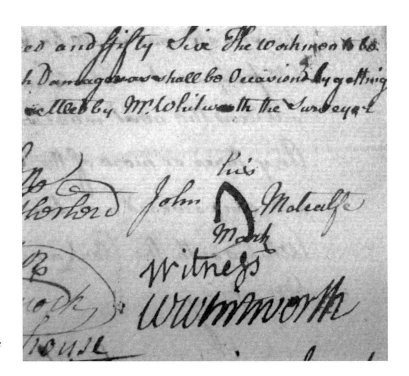

Blind Jack's mark upon a 1756 turnpike contract.

The trustees were so satisfied with his Harrogate-Harewood road – still a busy section of the A61 in use today – that they offered him another contract. This was at a meeting chaired by Lord Harewood, held at the Bowling Green in Chapeltown, which is now in the northern part of central Leeds. It included his agreement to lengthen the arch of Sheepscar Bridge by 10ft. For this and the road of a little over a mile they paid him 'near four hundred pounds'.[22]

Blind Jack was very much a Yorkshireman, but roads ignore all county boundaries, and his next contract was to take him over the border into Lancashire. This was for 4 miles of the road from Skipton to Colne. This he admits to have been one of his least successful projects:

> The materials were at a greater distance, and more difficult to be procured, than he expected; and a wet season coming on, made this a bad bargain; yet he completed it according to contract.[23]

The venture into Lancashire brought further financial disappointments. When he reached Colne he agreed to make another 2 miles of the road leading to Burnley. He completed this also, but made no profit. The trustees were very pleased with him, however, and offered him what was to prove a better contract, bringing him back into Yorkshire.

This, probably completed by the end of 1755, was for 2 miles of the road through Broughton as far as East Marton, to the west of Skipton. To this was added two more miles on the road from Skipton to Ilkley – through the village of Addingham and along the edge of Rombalds Moor, of which Ilkley Moor is the best-known part. For these last two pieces of work he received from the trustees, Mr Ingham of Burnley, and Mr Alcock of Skipton, a total of £1,350.[24]

Now he was back in his native county, John Metcalf went from strength to strength. He followed his work in the Ilkley area by turning his attention to the growing industrial area south of Leeds, mainly between Halifax and Wakefield. This had originally been turnpiked in the 1740s, but a new Act in 1755 authorised alterations and improvements. His first contract here was for 4 miles of the Halifax road from Mill Bridge through Bailiffe Bridge (or 'Belly Bridge', as Blind Jack knew it). There is interesting confirmation of this road in the minutes of the Wakefield-Halifax Turnpike Trust, where the meticulous nature of payment is evident:

> The Trustees have contracts with John Metcalfe to repair one mile from the Top of Birkby Lane towards Hightown before Michaelmass next according to the plan delivered at this Meeting by John Gott for Nineteen Shillings per Rood and when Thirty Roods are Completed to the Satisfaction of the Commissioners the same are to be measured off and twenty of them paid for and the other Ten to remain unpaid for as a Security for completing the rest effectually and so thro'out the rest of that Mile…

Further payments of £30, £50 and £70 are recorded, with a niggardly reference to 'one hundred and seventy pounds he had received before in full for one mile except three yards'.[25]

What is so interesting about this entry in the minutes is that it obviously constituted the contract itself, and is actually signed by Blind Jack – not with a cross, as we might have expected, but with a kind of flourish, testified by a witness to be 'John Metcalfe, his Mark.' (See previous page.)

In the account book it is also stated that the Revd John Lister of Shibden Hall, Halifax, made the following payments on behalf of the Trust towards the end of 1756:

> To John Metcalfe, on Acct. of work done on the Turnpike Road, and for which he stands to me accountable… £20. To John Metcalfe, on Acct of the work done on Turnpike Road from Halifax to Wakefield… £20.[26]

We are reminded of this today by the name 'Lister's Road', passing Shibden Hall, which Blind Jack resurfaced and perhaps realigned.[27]

In spite of an exceptionally wet summer, this work, as usual, was completed in the agreed time. He then moved across to Wakefield and made the 5 miles of road from there to Chickenley Beck, which is just outside Dewsbury. For this Halifax-Wakefield work he received a total of £1,200.

Blind Jack was now thoroughly established as a reputable builder of roads and ready to take on more ambitious projects, all capable of making him a wealthy man. Wakefield, eventually to become the administrative centre for the whole of the West Riding (until 1974), was in the second half of the eighteenth century a flourishing town, important as a centre of woollen manufacture, then coal mining, and dependent on good communication with the rest of Yorkshire. In 1756 the turnpike trustees, including Sir Rowland Winn, met in Wakefield to discuss the improvement of roads to Pontefract to the east and Doncaster further south. Metcalf was given contracts for 3 miles of the road between Hag Bridge and Pontefract, and for a mile and a half on the Doncaster road, from the Wakefield end, from Crofton to Foulby. Years later he apparently distinctly remembered the names of the trustees he dealt with, especially the treasurers for the various sections of the Turnpike Trust – Mr Allan Johnson and John Mills esq., both of Wakefield, for one section and

Blind Jack and his horse. (Peter Kearney)

Mr Valentine Stead and Mr William Cook for the others. From these four gentlemen he received a total of £6,400.[28]

This was an unprecedented sum for Blind Jack – more than four times the amount he received for the same distance of approximately 5 miles of the Harrogate-Harewood road. It was, in fact, by far the biggest single payment he ever received.

He does not tell us how much of this was profit, or how many men he employed on this work in the Wakefield area. But he had obviously done well enough to permit – if he wished – a more leisurely life in Knaresborough with Dolly and the children, perhaps with occasional visits to the Harrogate Spa, where he enjoyed his music, the more than occasional flutter, and drinking with his many friends.

Yet he was still only just over forty, full of vigour and ambition. And he was convinced he had a real vocation as a civil engineer. So he now committed himself fully to a programme of building roads – one that would occupy the next thirty-six years of his life.

Chapter Twelve

The Open Road: Profit and Loss

The next phase of Blind Jack's road-making would take him into parts that were wild and remote, the Pennine moors of Yorkshire, Lancashire and Derbyshire, the kind of territory evoked by the poet who wrote of his achievement on his headstone:

Twas his a guide's unerring aid to lend,
O'er trackless wastes to bid new roads extend.

One of his most challenging projects, some of it over unmarked terrain, was to work on the road that led over the bleak moorland of Standege, part of the road that ran westwards to the Lancashire border at Austerlands. This was, in fact, the most important route over the Pennines from Yorkshire to Lancashire, and not really superseded until the M62 was opened. The route over Standedge, in spite of being so exposed, was a natural choice, because at 1,300ft it was the lowest point of the watershed. Jack heard of the advertisement inviting tenders for this new road, and went down to the meeting at Huddersfield. Here he offered his services to the trustees, who included Sir John Kaye, Colonel Radcliffe and Squire Farrer.

A meeting had previously been held at the George Inn, Huddersfield, in June 1755 to consider an application to Parliament for a 'Turnpike Road from Wakefield thro' Huddersfield, to Austerlands, to join the Turnpike from thence to Manchester'.[1] As a result of this meeting the application had been made, and a Turnpike Act passed in 1758, this stressing that a road was needed, adequate to carry, not just pack horses, but wheeled vehicles. John Metcalf now came to an agreement with the trusteees, eventually constructing a total of 21 miles of the road. This was a major undertaking, including the building of bridges and toll houses, and at one point he would be employing around 400 men.[2] It meant that he had to move from Knaresborough to stay in the area for many months, the local tradition being that he used as his headquarters the White Hart inn in Towngate, said to be the oldest building in Marsden, no longer standing.

The bold, risk-taking nature of Blind Jack in tackling such an enterprise in this wild countryside struck me forcibly when I visited this area some years ago. It was on a day course organised by the University of Bradford which included a visit to the Countryside Centre at Marsden, at the entrance to the Standedge Tunnel.[3] Here we saw a map of the area to the south-west of Marsden showing sections of the first turnpike road built by Blind Jack in 1759-60, starting from near the tunnel entrance, and going south of Pule Hill and over Thieves Clough to Diggle – and to Delph, where, at the Swan Inn, Blind Jack traditionally stayed, and on to Austerlands. It also showed the second turnpike he built, slightly to the south of the first route, in 1781.

It was when we went out onto this area of barren, windswept moorland – on a cold and clouded afternoon – that I realised what hardships he and his men must have endured. The land was not only hilly, but had a characteristic feature of cloughs – ravines or small, steep-sided valleys. Yet we were able to walk along a good unmetalled road laid down by Blind Jack, still retaining one or two of the milestones perhaps set up more than a couple of centuries before.

Almost as soon as he started, Jack ran into a serious difficulty which led to a dispute with the trustees. The surveyor had planned the road to cross the Pule and Standedge Common, which meant that it had to negotiate what Jack discovered to be 'deep marshes', a half-mile stretch, which has been identified by a later writer as the part (exactly that distance) 'between Mount Bar… and Gilbert's', which an O.S. map of 1854 shows to contain two adjacent slades or marshes.4

Jack told the trustees that to take the road directly across marshes of this kind would be far too expensive. They replied that they wanted the road to follow the surveyor's route, and that they would make sure he would suffer no financial loss over the work. All he needed to do, they said, was dig down into the quagmire until they reached more solid ground beneath. Blind Jack, as was his custom, had already done his sums:

> Metcalf, on calculting that each marsh, upon an average, being three yards deep, and fourteen broad, would make two hundred and ninety four solid yards of earth in every road, which, to have carried away, would have been extremely tedious and expensive – and not only so, but that the road lying East and West, would fill with snow in winter, (as it usually falls in that direction, when the wind is in the North) – argued the point privately with the surveyor and several of the gentleman, but they all seemed immoveable in their former opinion.5

As neither side would give in, a public meeting was called. Jack, seeing there would be no point in holding a contest with them, told them he would not trespass further on their time. He would make the road they required – but by his own method. If it did not prove a good road, then he would, at his own expense, make it again, following their own proposed method.

This they agreed to, and he set to work with a gang of sixty men on this difficult section of the road – one of six separate sections that he had started. As they worked, water was running across their excavations, and much time was spent in digging drains. Another difficulty was that the horses and wagons, heavy with stones, kept sinking into the soft ground. Added to this were the complaints and jeers of the pack-horse cloth merchants, on their way to Huddersfield. According to Samuel Smiles they mocked Metcalf and 'declared that he and his men would some day have to be dragged out of the bog by the hair of their heads'.6

But Metcalf mastered this bog, just like the previous ones. Instead of digging out all the waterlogged soil, as the trustees wanted, he applied his already well-tried method of taking the road down to the usual depth, and then laying a foundation of tough-rooted heather (gorse is not mentioned here) before adding the stones and gravel.

> He ordered his men to pull and bind heather, or ling, in round bundles that they could span with their hands, and directed them to lay it on the intended road, by placing the bundles in rows, and laying another upon each, pressing them well down; as the carts were obliged to come on and go off at one end, he always kept it covered in this manner, with ling for the carriages to turn upon. He then brought broad-wheeled carts, and began to lead stone and gravel for covering. When the first load was brought and laid on, and the horses had gone off in safety, the company huzza'd from surprise.7

In his account of how he got a road across the marshes he admits that, at the time, he tried to keep his heather-foundation method as secret as possible. There were rival road-makers who would certainly borrow the idea if they knew how successful it was. Giving his memories to the public in 1795, however, he felt it was now time to make it known 'as it may be useful to any person who chuses to pursue the plan'. Some did – though it is not clear whether or not they got the idea from John Metcalf. The best-known example is of George Stephenson who used this method to carry his railway line over marshes in 1830.[8]

Metcalf's method of taking a road over boggy ground, though not patented, is considered by writers on civil engineering to have been original, and not previously recorded.[9] Certainly, the roads he made in this way were very successful. Looking back to his work in 1759, and the dozen years which followed it, he is able to say without any fear of contradiction:

> They completed the whole of this length, which was about half a mile; and it was so particularly fine, that any person might have gone over it in winter, unshod, without being wet. This piece of road needed no repairs for twelve years afterwards, but the other parts of the road wanted repairing immediately after.[10]

It is a pity that isolated comments like this, and brief descriptions of how he worked, are all he chose to give us. This comment is followed, for example, by an observation that just happens to occur to him, to the effect that his way of taking a road over soft clay is to lay down a foundation, not of heather, but of sand. A systematic account of his procedure would have been of great historical value, but because of his blindness – and in the early years because of caution about giving his secrets away to rivals – it is understandable that we have no Metcalf manual of road building.

Having finished the first 9 miles in the agreed ten months, he went on to make 3 miles of road from Standedge to Thurston Clough, 6 miles from Sir John Kaye's estate to Huddersfield, then a mile and a half to Longroyd. During the course of his work he also built no fewer then ten small bridges, mostly to carry the road over the streams that ran in the bottom of the cloughs: four bridges with a span of 24ft, and six with a span of only 9ft – more what we would call culverts. A neat little bridge I particularly enjoyed seeing – after walking on a stretch of Blind Jack's road, with its original surface, undisguised by tarmac – was the one across Thieves Clough. This would be one of those he built on this wet ground without any solid stone foundation.

> In the building of bridges, where the foundations were bad, he laid on a sufficient thickness of ling where it could be got, otherwise of wheat straw; he next laid planks five inches thick, with square mortises cut through; and driving in a number of piles, he made the foundation secure. He then laid springs for the arch upon the planks, which caused all to settle regularly when the weight came on. And tho' he built many arches, of different sizes, by taking this method, none ever fell.[11]

He had to bargain with the trustees to get £300 for extra work in the marshes, but his total payment, which covered the building of bridges and three toll houses, and 21 miles of road, was £4,500.

His success in building the toll houses led him to break out into yet another sideline – the building of a substantial dwelling house. This he undertook as a kind of tail piece to his work on the Wakefield-Austerlands road while he was still in the Huddersfield area. Having managed to get free stone from a quarry on land belonging to Sir John Ramsden, he set about building a house for a gentleman by the name of Marmaduke

Hebdin. This was no small toll house, but a small mansion 'nine yards wide, twenty-three yards long, and 21ft from the foundation to the square of the building; it had twenty chimneys or pipes.'[12] To organise the construction of such a house, as a little extra to the big road-building project he had just completed, would have been remarkable enough for any man. We have to remind ourselves, once again, that this inexhaustible workaholic was blind.

His building of Marmaduke Hebdin's 'Folly Hall', as it was later called, is confirmed by a little-known document which relates to his work in the Huddersfield area and gives remarkable insight into the stubborn and argumentative side of Blind Jack's character. This is the day book of John Turner, a sparsely worded diary kept by an attorney who lived in Huddersfield, residing at the George Inn from 1736, and later moving, when married, to nearby Hopton. As well as practising as an attorney, Turner engaged to some extent in trade, in Huddersfield in particular, organising the 'leading' (transporting in wagons) of coal and other heavy loads – including the stone that Blind Jack required for his road building. So we find that he records in his day book that he had spent time with Blind Jack at the George inn at Huddersfield and been given a contract by him:

12.6.1760   I at Marsden. 1d spt [1 penny spent] with blind Jack Metcalfe at Geo Huddersfield, 2s & ordd me & 2 carts & 4 horses to begin turnpike tomorrow at 6s per day.
16.6.1760   Rd Shaw & I to Blackmoorfoot & led stones all day.
17.6.1760   Rd Shaw, coal & 3 horses at Marsden, Jno Metcalfe finds meat for all.[13]

Then comes the entry which shows that John Turner, an apparently respectable and mild-mannered man and a regular churchgoer, got into an argument with Blind Jack over his bad-tempered refusal to pay him on time and provide the agreed amount:

18.7.1760   Spt [spent] with Robert Broadley & Dan Smith at Robert Turners after we had been to see if blind Jack would pay us & wd not.
29.10.1760   Spent at Marriotts to get pd of Blind Jack 3d. but none. Turnpike meeting.
22.12.1760   Spent at Marriotts at Turnpike meeting to get pd of Blind Jno Metcalfe & abused me & set me at defiance.[14]

Blind Jack coughed up payment in the New Year – but not the full amount to which Turner felt he was entitled:

12.1.1761   Recd of John Metcalfe £1. 3. 6. But wronged me of 2 days.

The following year Turner notes that Blind Jack had sufficient cash to beat him in the buying of a cow. Then, it seems, friendly relations were resumed and further contracts were agreed:

1.5.1762   Spt with J. Gibson at J B jnr abt buying white cow & blind Jack Metcalfe bot her at £4.10.6.
18.10.1762   Spt at Geo meeting blind Jack Metcalfe about going to turnpike at Out Coat Bank.
9.12.1762   Blind Jack Metcalfe, son Jno [Turner's son, John], cart & 3 horses at turnpike 2nd day.[15]

While he was working away from home in the area to the south-west of Huddersfield the distance between there and Knaresborough meant that he could certainly not have commuted by horse. At first, we can assume that he would have made occasional return visits to see his wife and family, but any long separation from Dolly is not consonant with the various indications and expressions of his affection for her, nor to the reference to his absences being only 'occasional'.[16] It is unfortunate that we have no account of how John Metcalf managed to keep his undoubtedly happy marriage intact during these years of road-making. Either he did not care to talk to his amanuensis about his personal affairs, or such information as he gave was edited out of the final draft as being of little consequence to readers. We can be sure, however, that Dolly and the children moved from Knaresborough to stay in the vicinity of his roadworks some time during his Wakefield-Austerlands project, started in 1759.

Evidence for this is in a curious letter – indeed, the only surviving letter – dictated by Blind Jack. It is quoted as 'an extract from a letter to a friend' by the Victorian topographical writer, Edmund Bogg. He does not identify Blind Jack's friend, or say how he came by the letter, but if we allow for the stylistic changes made by Jack's scribe it reads convincingly enough – especially as it gives details of two important turnpike trustees mentioned in his printed memoirs. It starts by referring to his agreement to make 'between 20 and 30 miles' of the Wakefield-Manchester turnpike, his employment of 'about four hundred men', spread out in companies a few miles distant from each other, and then comes the first reference to Dolly:

> I stationed myself and family, with a number of horses and carts, at a place called Lepton, near the road-side, about five miles east of Huddersfield and eight west of Wakefield.[17]

From this it is clear enough that once he had moved away from the Knaresborough-Harrogate area to do his road building, Blind Jack's family moved around with him. The only substantial accommodation in Lepton at that time was the White Horse inn (since rebuilt), a place which stands, as he says, near the road he was working on. The assumption that the inn was his base is strengthened by the fact that parts of his original road can be seen nearby, with culverts taking the water underneath.[18]

The authenticity of his letter gains some confirmation from the anecdote he now tells about one of the trustees, Colonel Radcliffe, captain of a company in the militia. Jack, being an old militia soldier himself, went frequently to his house, where a new hall was being built. One day, he says in the letter, he found a coach standing idle in the courtyard. The colonel told him he had no use for it, though it had cost his father a hundred guineas.

> I told him, as he had no lady, I would buy it off him for my lady. After a good many words betwixt us, I agreed to it for four guineas, though it was worth four or five times the money.

This last bit of boasting fits in perfectly with the many other references we have to Blind Jack's skill as a bargainer. Also fitting in so well with his concern over criticism that Dolly had married beneath her, and that her parents had never been happy with her lower station in life, he takes pleasure in making another boast:

> Then we proceeded home to Lepton, and the Sunday following yoked six cart-horses to the coach, and told my wife she should ride in a coach and six of her own. Though her relatives reflected on her marriage, yet she has risen to a greater pitch than any of her generation before her.[19]

He adds to this the story about Sir John Kaye, another trustee, who lived a mile away from Lepton, at Grange Hall. 'He being a good-natured gentleman', he says, 'and often being free in talking to me', he jokingly invited him to accompany them in his chaise when they went for a drive in their coach and six. He rounds off his story about this grand coach by saying that he told Dolly that if they kept it they would need 'new liveries for servants, and new harnesses for six horses'. So he eventually broke up the coach, making good use of the leather and iron, and transferring the wheels to two of

Rainow Bridge, built in 1770.

his carts. The final sentence is in the writer's literary English, but it translates the sort of whimsical comment Jack would have made in his earthy dialect: 'I can't say but it caused rather a flatness in my lady, to see her splendid equipage so suddenly demolished'.

This letter is sufficient indication, then, that in the early 1760s Blind Jack had a family base at Lepton. The most interesting of his children was his second, Tabitha, born in 1742, and now of marriageable age. About this time she met David Jackson, a cotton manufacturer from the Stockport area, and they were married on the 7 December 1767 at Knaresborough.[20] Their first two children were baptised in 1768 and 1773 at Mottram in Longendale and they then moved a little nearer Stockport to their home, Spout House (still to be seen), at Gee Cross, Hyde. Here, at the nearby Unitarian Chapel, their next children were baptised – Tabitha (1777), Dolly (1779) and John (1785).[21] So it is likely that Blind Jack and Dolly senior stayed with this Stockport branch of the family at Mottram and Gee Cross, or had a house in this area, during the years when Jack was working close by, taking his roads from Yorkshire into Lancashire, Cheshire and Derbyshire.

His next contract, after finishing the big house near Huddersfield, was to make the road from Doctor Lane Head (misheard by Peck as Dock Lane Head) to Ashton-under-Lyne. From there he worked southwards, towards Stockport, and to the north-east as far as Mottram. The project extended more than 18 miles, involving several teams working in different parts, each with its own horses and carts. The winter was so severe that he lost twenty horses, but philosophically remarked that 'horse-leather had been dear a long time, but he hoped now to reduce the price.' To this comment, typical of his dry humour, is added his reminiscence:

> Notwithstanding this misfortune, he completed the whole, including a great number of drains and arches, which were all done to the satisfaction of the trustees and surveyor; and received for the work four thousand five hundred pounds.[22]

In 1770 he started work on another 8 miles of road from Chapel-le-Frith in Derbyshire, running south-west to Macclesfield in Cheshire. On this stretch he encountered a serious setback near Whaley Bridge. This was the problem of building a bridge where the road crossed the River Dern at the village of Rainow. It is interesting to see how fully and carefully he dictated what he remembered about this bridge – one of which he was, in the end, very proud. It is almost as though he knew it would always be known locally as 'Blind Jack's Bridge' – and that in modern times it would receive a national award.

When he came to dig out the foundations for the bridge he discovered thick clay about a yard deep, in which 'whick springs appeared' (this would be *wick* in the Yorkshire dialect sense of 'lively, fast-flowing'). So he instructed his men to bore with rods to a depth of several yards – only to find that more springs appeared. He wanted to apply his usual method of making a base of bundles of gorse and heather, but there was none of this near. He decided to try, as a substitute, strong straw. With typical caution about having his methods stolen by rivals, he went to two of his labourers 'whom he could confide in for keeping a secret', and asked them to get him 'a few threaves of good wheat straw'. (A threave, or thrave was used in dialect to mean a bundle or stook of corn, straw etc) and bring them – at dead of night – to where the foundations for the bridge had been dug out. Twenty-five years later he recalls, in remarkable detail, how he managed this awkward construction:

> They did so, and digged about two foot deep, then laid the straw, about half a yard thick, then had wood planks about seven inches thick, proper holes being made through them, and to be tapered; the planks was to break joint, so as one end was to go by another; likewise piles shod with iron, five yards long, with their heads tapered, so that they would drive into the planks but not to go through, then a course of stones, five feet long and seven inchesthick, to be laid upon these planks, and then another course of the same to be laid upon them, but so laid that they might break the joints; the arch was sprung of that, so that every thing settled together and one thing could not leave another, being similar to whey crushed out of cheese until it come to a solid body. This bridge has been built thirty years, and the foundation has never cost one penny in repairs; any body who chuses to make use of this method will find it infallible for a bridge.[23]

Once again, having spoken of his secrecy, he now feels that, at this interval of time, he can safely share his methods with others.

The Rainow Bridge, built in 1770, lasted much longer than the thirty years mentioned by Blind Jack. A fine single-span sandstone arch, it carried traffic safely for nearly 230 years, until it was decided to strengthen and widen it so it could easily carry the 40 tonne vehicles permitted on the A5002. This was done discreetly, one side of the bridge being dismantled and rebuilt a little further out. Using extra stone from a local quarry and also traditional building methods, the original appearance of the bridge was faithfully preserved, and when we look at it today, although the lighter colour of the newer stone can be detected underneath, the bridge looks exactly as it must have done when first built. It is not surprising that in May 1999 Cheshire County Council received the national Civic Trust Award for their excellent refurbishment of Blind Jack's Bridge.[24]

For the 8 miles of this Chapel-le-Frith to Macclesfield road, including the Rainow Bridge and another small bridge, John Metcalf received from the trustees, Mr Stafford and his sons, of Macclesfield, £2,000.[25]

At this point in the printed version of his memoirs there is confusion and repetition, with distances and payments mentioned, but no dates. However, Blind Jack's next projects included 10 miles of road between Huddersfield and Wakefield, for which he received £2,500 from 'Mr Fenton, Attorney at Law, Greenside near Huddersfield', and a further £3,500 from the same attorney for 10 miles of a road from Huddersfield to High Moor.[26] Between 1777 and 1778 he was making the 8 miles of road between Huddersfield and

Halifax, via Grimscar, for which he would receive £2,700, including the provision of drains, arches and walls.[27]

In the midst of this work, and at around sixty years of age still in the prime of life, Jack was a very worried man. Dolly, only the same age, was in declining health, and what was thought to be some kind of rheumatism flared up into a fatal illness. She had been staying at Spout House, Gee Cross, with her daughter Tabitha and the family, and seems to have spent the last days of her life in Stockport itself, where she sought medical advice and treatment, but in vain. Jack briefly makes mention of:

> …the much-loved Partner of his cares, whom he had brought into Cheshire, and left at Stockport, that she might avail herself of the medical advice of a person there, famed for the cure of Rheumatic complaints, of which description her's was thought to be. But human aid proving ineffectual, she there died, in the summer of 1778, after thirty-nine years of conjugal felicity, which was never interrupted but by her illness or his occasional absence.[28]

Dolly's funeral took place at Stockport parish church – in April, rather than summer – and she was buried in the churchyard. I have not been able to find her headstone, but the epitaph was copied from it by a Victorian local historian as follows:

> In Memory of Dorothy, Wife of John Metcalf,
> who died April 12th, 1778, aged 61 Years.
> At Harrogate in Yorkshire I was born,
> But now my Body lies under this Stone.
> To you I've left Behind it's sure to be
> your Body when in dust will lie the same as me.
> take care in time to obtain a happy fate,
> and don't neglect for fear it may be too late.
> All you that come these lines to see,
> prepair in time to follow me.[29]

John and Dorothy Metcalf had a happy marriage, which lasted until just a year before they would have been able to celebrate their Ruby Wedding. There is a real poignancy in the words 'thirty-nine years of conjugal felicity' – not how Jack would have expressed it in the original Yorkshire dialect, but the equivalent in a sonorous latinism, typical of the late eighteenth century. Also typical of the period is the way he adds to the mention of Dolly's death yet another reference to the difference in their social standing, and how he had done his very best for her, and ensured that 'she had no unreasonable desires to gratify'.[30]

It goes without saying that Jack must have been utterly grief-stricken by the loss of the girl he had eloped with, and to whom he had been utterly devoted ever since. For all these years she had looked after him, as well as the children, giving the little personal attentions especially appreciated by someone who is blind, and supporting him in his work both by keeping his accounts and giving him unfailing encouragement.

We can imagine him in that churchyard at Stockport, accompanied by his grieving family, feeling his way with his stick to the headstone, then reading the newly-cut inscription with his finger-tips…What could he do without Dolly? How could he go on?

He remembered how proud he was of all he had achieved, and decided he would do what she would have wanted him to do. He would return to his roads.

Chapter Thirteen

Towards the End of the Road

Bereft of his beloved Dolly, Blind Jack now went back to his road-making. It must have required tremendous courage to go out on the road each day knowing that 'the much-loved Partner of his cares' was not there for him to return to. But at least he would have had a home in the Stockport area, where Tabitha and her family looked after him. With David Jackson's cotton business and the savings from his own considerable income, Jack, now 61, could have nursed his grief – if he had wished – in comfortable retirement. Yet he was not only a man of action, always on the move, but also understood, like so many who are bereaved, that there is a real therapy in work, especially work like his, which kept him fully occupied, and provided him with the prospect of tangible accomplishment. The completion of a section of good road, to be used by countless appreciative travellers, would still be a source of satisfaction and consolation.

No doubt because of the emotion aroused as he recalled his bereavement, together with his traumatised memory, Jack's account at this point again becomes confused and repetitive, the amanuensis obviously having done his best to make sense of it.

Though we cannot be sure of the order of events – since no dates are given – it seems likely that the work he went back to was the completion of the Huddersfield and Halifax commission, which was followed by starting work on the road from Congleton to the Red Bull, taking him from Cheshire into Staffordshire. This included the building of drains, arches and walls, and for the total work he was paid £3,500 by Mr John Smith, a Stockport attorney.[1]

Vague about the dates and order of his undertakings, Blind Jack sometimes remembers and relates a detailed experience that lightened the routine work of road building. There is a curious instance of this in his long account of his dealings with a man named Warburton, whom he met at the Swan Inn in Congleton. He describes him as 'a capital farmer', this adjective signifying that he used his funds for speculation. He lived about a mile from Congleton, said Jack, and 'was remarkable for sporting large sums in various ways.'

Warburton approached him, saying that he understood he played cards. 'Sometimes, but not often,' replied Metcalf, concealing his vast experience of handling cards. The farmer offered to play him for up to £10 in the best of five of the game known as 'put' – an old card-game for two, three or four players, similar to the game of 'nap'.[2] Jack recalls that he would have gladly played with this man, but he realised he was at a disadvantage, partly because he was so preoccupied with his turnpike work, but mainly because he had no sighted friends present in the inn to see that there was fair play (or perhaps give him coded hints in the course of the game!). He therefore declined, but jokingly kept the possibility open:

> I have not now time, but if you will meet me here this day fortnight I will play you the best of five games – for a leg of mutton, four pennyworth of cabbage, and five shillings worth of punch.[3]

The farmer, pleased at the prospect of playing cards with the famous Metcalf, agreed, his money being deposited with the landlord.

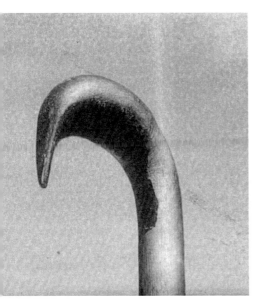

The handle of Blind Jack's cherry-wood stick.

A drawing from life by J.R. Smith, January 1795, when Blind Jack was seventy-seven (the age has been adjusted by the publishers).

During the interval Warburton spread the story of his engagement to play with a blind man and, thinking it a good joke, invited many of his friends to the entertainment. Metcalf came at the time fixed, having first engaged a friend from Buxton to accompany him, whose chief business it was to see that his adversary did not play tricks with the cards.

The farmer tried to get Jack to play for serious money, but at first he refused, made more jokes, then borrowed a fiddle from the landlord. He played a few of his lively tunes on this, and the farmer, now unsure of what he had taken on, asked him what he meant by this surprising musical interlude. Jack, seizing the opportunity for another of his puns, replied that it was: 'To enable you to tell your children that when you played with a blind man you played to some tune.'[4]

They then went into a large adjoining room, where they were followed by a great crowd of people, including two justices of the peace and several clergymen, all curious to see what the blind card player could do.

Metcalf won the first two games, Warburton the third. Still refusing to play for money, Jack went on to win the rubber. Yet more money was put on the table, but he agreed only to play for liquor, and this was to be for the benefit of the crowd. He eventually defeated the farmer so soundly that, sensing he had wanted to boast he had beaten a blind man, he started to joke again about his 'childish manner of playing' and told him that when the road work should cease for the Christmas holidays, he would come to his house, and teach him to play like a man.[5]

Blind Jack won such a quantity of liquor for the spectators that some of them were drinking there until five o'clock in the morning. Warburton himself got drunk, he tells us, and before leaving admitted that 'of twenty-two fine cows, he would rather have lost the best than have been beaten so publickly'.

It is greatly to Metcalf's credit that, realising he would now have many people wanting to gamble with him, and that this could distract him from his work, he went to Mr Rolle, the surveyor, and promised him £5 if he should ever play cards during the next eighteen months, the time allotted for the finishing of the road. Rolle was pleased to agree to this, and publicly presented him with a token sixpence to show his side of the agreement, which was never apparently broken by Jack.

It was while Blind Jack was working in the area to the south of Manchester that he was visited and interviewed by an important witness, who was able to testify both to his outstanding accomplishments and the fact that these were all the more remarkable because of his undoubted total blindness. This man was George Bew, a member of the Manchester Literary and Philosophical Society, for which he produced a paper, read on the 17 April 1782, entitled 'Observations on Blindness, and on the Other Senses to supply the Loss of Sight.' As part of his research he made several visits to see Blind Jack in action, and interviewed him on his life and methods. Taking him as an illustration because he was 'well-known in this neighbourhood', Bew starts by mentioning his early work as a wagoner and occasionally 'as a guide on intricate roads during the night, or when tracks were covered with snow', and then goes on to make the first public announcement of John Metcalf's essential claim to fame:

> Strange as this may appear to those who can see, the employment he has since undertaken is still more extraordinary: it is one of the last to which we could suppose a blind man would ever turn his attention. His present occupation is that of a projector and surveyor of highways in difficult and mountainous parts.[6]

This, he continues, is something he has observed himself. What follows is an significant piece of evidence from an external source, as distinct from Metcalf's own claims or the accounts of turnpike trusts. This part of Bew's paper needs to be quoted in full:

> With the assistance only of a long staff, I have several times met this man traversing the roads, ascending precipices, exploring valleys, and investigating their several extents, forms, and situations, so as to answer his designs in the best manner. The plans which he designs, and the estimates he makes, are done in a method peculiar to himself, and which he cannot well convey the meaning of to others.
>
> His abilities, in this respect, are, nevertheless, so great, that he finds constant employment. Most of the roads over the Peak in Derbyshire have been altered by his directions; particularly those in the vicinity of Buxton: and he is, at this time, constructing a new one, betwixt Wilmslow and Congleton, with a view to open a communication to the great London road, without being obliged to pass over the mountains.[7]

After delivering the paper to the meeting, Bew met Blind Jack once again, while he was working on the Congleton to Wilmslow road. In the printed version of his lecture he adds a footnote about the discussion he then had with him:

> Amongst other conversation, I made some inquiries respecting this new road. It was really astonishing to hear with what accuracy he described the courses, and the nature of the different soils, through which it was conducted. Having mentioned to him a boggy piece of ground it passed through, he observed, that 'that was the only place he had doubts concerning, and that he was apprehensive they had, contrary to his directions, been too sparing of their materials'.[8]

The essential purpose of Bew's paper is to show to what a remarkable extent the other senses may be used to compensate for the loss of sight. He points out that it is not just the perceptions of hearing and touch, for example, but the way these are stored in the memory. 'It is chiefly by the assistance of memory', he says, 'that the blind acquire the exquisite advantages derived from other senses'. They are better able to concentrate on this remembered data because they are 'undistracted by the never-ceasing variety which is always present to the organs of vision, when awake'.9

Of the various examples he gives to support his line of argument, the strongest is that of John Metcalf, who gave him his personal explanation of how he was able to do what he did. Once again, we do not have the original Yorkshire style of Blind Jack, but an educated man's refined paraphrase of it. And this is as near as we come to a personal statement of how Jack understood his astonishing ability:

> The blind unlettered projector of roads could reply to me, when I expressed myself surprized at the accuracy of his discriminations, 'that there was nothing surprizing in the matter. 'You, Sir', says he, 'can have recourse to your eyesight whenever you want to see or examine anything; whereas, I have only my memory to trust to.' There is one advantage, however, he remarked, that he possessed. 'The readiness with which you view an object at pleasure prevents the necessity of fixing the ideas of it deeply in your mind, and the impressions, in general, become quickly obliterated. On the contrary, the information I possess, being acquired with greater difficulty, is, on that very account, so firmly fixed on the memory, as to be almost indelible.10

It would have been even better if George Bew had managed to persuade Blind Jack to appear before the Society to give a first-hand account and answer questions. Perhaps he thought of this, and his request was declined. Jack had no interest in academics, and would not have wanted to appear before them as a specimen to be scrutinised. Moreover, he was far too busy completing his contracts to be able to travel to Manchester in the cause of philosophical and scientific investigation.

One break which he did allow from his work in the area south of Manchester was a return visit in 1781 to Knaresborough. This was not just to renew old contacts with relations and friends, but to accept a contract to build the turnpike between Knaresborough and Wetherby, which lay on the Great North Road. For this comparatively short and easy road of a little over 6 miles, going through Little Ribston and Kirk Deighton, he says he received about £380 – not a large sum, when we consider that his work here included the building of a toll house, still to be seen. This cannot have been the total payment, however. In his disordered way he elsewhere refers to receiving 'for part of the road from Knaresborough to Wetherby, about six hundred pounds from Mr Ogden of Knaresborough, being Clerk and Treasurer.'11

An interesting feature of Blind Jack's work on this road so near his old home in Knaresborough is that he seems to have taken particular care with it, and he so impressed the trustees with the fine quality of the toll house he had built at Kirk Deighton that they decided to pay him more than he had asked. With the list of signatories headed by the Revd Thomas Collins, the gentlemen agreed as follows:

> …that the Treasurer do pay John Metcalf the sum of Seventy Pounds for the building of a Toll House at Kirk Deighton Lane End for the benefit of the Trustees… being Four Pounds and Ten Shillings more than his Contract for doing the same. This additional sum is allowed on Account of his having finished this Work well, and in a Superior mode to his Contract.12

The significance of this statement – lying forgotten in a dusty book of minutes in the archives – is that it confirms the reputation of Blind Jack as a man who finished his contracts on or before time, and always to the highest standard. A further indication of the esteem in which he was held is that, in the same order book, the Trustees agree to allow the 'Old Toll House' (nearer Wetherby) to remain standing 'for the Sole and only Use of John Metcalf of Knaresborough, Yeoman, and his Heirs'.[13]

Back in the Stockport area, he began to take more interest in the cotton business run by his son-in-law, David Jackson. He retained a good knowledge of cloth and clothing from the days when he had traded in the goods he brought from Scotland to Yorkshire in the period following his return from Culloden. Perhaps, now that he was in his late sixties, he was looking for work that was less physically demanding than road building, and he decided to branch out into serious textile speculation. He first paid for the construction of six spinning jennies and a carding machine. He then bought a quantity of cotton, which he had spun into yarn. In spite of help and advice from his family he made a loss on this, but he was determined not to be beaten, and tried again:

> Then Metcalf got looms, and other implements proper for weaving calicoes, jeans, and velverets: for having made the cotton business an object of particular attention, he was become very well acquainted with the various branches of it. He got a quantity of calicoes whitened and printed, his velverets cut, dyed, etc. and having spun up all his cotton, he set off with about eight hundred yards of finished goods, intending to sell them in Yorkshire, which he did at Knaresborough and in the neighbourhood; and his son-in-law was to employ his jennies until he came back.[14]

Blind Jack's exceptional memory not only served him well as he handled physical things, from road-making items such as his viameter to the textile machinery and the finished products, but also in accurate recall of earlier situations. On the return journey to Stockport, via Marsden, he remembered the work he had done here in 1759. It was a happy coincidence for him that when he reached Marsden he heard there was to be a meeting to discuss the making of a mile and half of road and the building of a bridge. He could not resist attending the meeting, at which he agreed with the trustees to undertake the work.

This project may have given him a certain satisfaction – the feeling that he was re-living his younger days by working in Marsden again. But it was to prove the first of two unprofitable ventures which must have made him realise that it was time he brought his road-making to an end. This short road, known as the Coach Road, was to avoid a steep hill, but the ground over which he had to bring his vehicles was very swampy, and the weather particularly wet. He completed the bridge – known as Ottiwell's Bridge – a span of 12 yards, 9 yards broad. For the whole work he received £1,000, but this was far from sufficient to cover his expenses.[15]

It is to this unfortunate period that I think we can assign an undated story collected by William Grainge. This records a rare instance of Blind Jack being in dispute with his men. Because of the wet weather that had disrupted work on the Standedge road, he tells us, Jack had not been able to pay his gangs of workmen at the time agreed. So they took him to court, and he was brought before the Huddersfield magistrates for default of payment:

> The magistrates told him he 'ought to have provided against a rainy day'. Jack promptly rejoined that he had provided for one rainy day, but, unfortunately for him, two or more rainy days had come together.[16]

Writers have guessed that this second Marsden project was undertaken as early as 1781, but we know that it was completed just before a return to Knaresborough, precisely dated by the historian, Ely Hargrove, who shows how Metcalf was still held in the highest esteem in the town, and comments in the fourth edition of his *History*, published soon after the visit.[17]

> This extraordinary man was at Knaresborough, his native place, in June 1788, being just returned from finishing a piece of road, and constructing a bridge over a rivulet at Marsden, near Huddersfield, in Yorkshire, being then in the 71st year of his age, healthy and strong.[18]

The second unprofitable contract was secured in 1789, when he heard there were many sections of turnpike to be made in Lancashire. He undertook to make the part between Bury and Haslingden, then on to Accrington, with a branch to Blackburn, an area of especially bad roads, described by the much-travelled evangelist, John Wesley, the previous year as 'sufficient to lame any horse, and shake any carriage to pieces.'[19]

This was a much more ambitious project, especially for a blind man in his seventies, and covered at least sixteen difficult miles. It was to be his last piece of road-making, and his account of it makes melancholy reading, referring to the exceptional difficulty of the terrain, the changed economic circumstances, with higher wages, competition from 'the navigation' (i.e. the canal builders) and yet more wet weather:

> There were such hollows to fill, and hills to be taken down, to form the level, as was never done before: in several of the hollows the walls were ten yards high, before the battlements were put on the top. He had two summers allowed to finish this work in; but the trade in Lancashire being brisk, made wages very high, and the navigation at that time cutting through the country so employed the men, that it was a very difficult matter to procure a sufficiency of hands. The first summer the rains were so perpetual, that he lost about two hundred pounds; but in the next he completed the whole work, and received by the hands of Mr Carr, of Blackburn, three thousand five hundred pounds; and, after all, was forty pounds loser by it.[20]

Although this account of his very last piece of road-making sounds like a dismal conclusion to his career as a civil engineer, Blind Jack was long remembered in East Lancashire for his 'mirth and joviality… his curly locks and ruddy complexion' and the fact that he was a great raconteur and 'the life and soul of any company'. His base in Bury was the Ship inn, where the magistrates held court. There is a tradition that one of them:

> …complained that the bed of the ford over the River Irwell had become so dislocated that he had nearly been thrown from his stumbling horse. When he was returning four hours later, it had been repaired by Blind Jack and his road-makers without charge of any kind.[21]

He had apparently used four of his men to repair the bed of the ford, and later superseded this by building over the Irwell the fine double-arched Ewood Bridge.[22, 23]

In 1792 Blind Jack, at last laying aside his viameter, left Tabitha's home at Gee Cross, returned to Yorkshire, and came to live with his other married daughter, Ellen Ingleson, on a farm in Spofforth, a pleasant village 4 miles to the south of Knaresborough. This was not because, at the age of seventy-five, he was a frail valetudinarian, in need of somebody to look after him. On the contrary, he was still fit and active, and simply needed a comfortable home as his base for semi-retirement.

Spofforth possesses the fine parish church of All Saints', with some Norman work and interesting monuments, and also the ruins of Spofforth Castle, a seat of the Percy family, dismantled during the Civil War. It is surrounded by good farming country, and this gave Blind Jack the opportunity to try his hand at something new – trading in hay, and later wood:

> He bought hay to sell again, measuring the stacks with his arms, and having learnt the height, he could readily tell what number of square yards were contained, from five to one hundred pounds value.[24]

He made similar estimates with trees he bought and sold for wood, a feat similar to the one previously mentioned in connection with the Cowthorpe Oak.

The farm where he lived – still standing until about 1913 – was situated near the centre of the village, conveniently close to church and pub (see p. 46). But Blind Jack's wanderlust meant that he could not stay there for long periods. He had to be on the move, on foot, or on his horse, seeing his many friends in this part of Yorkshire.

In the first place, he frequently visited his old haunts. In Knaresborough another eccentric character styling himself 'Sir' Thomas Hill was now attracting visitors to his House in the Rock, or Fort Montague, completed in 1791, printing his own bank notes and firing cannon from his battlements. This no doubt suggested to Metcalf that he, too, could make money out of the new tourist trade based on Harrogate, and he already had an eye on another small business project which would exploit his popularity with the many spa visitors. Here he was surrounded by well wishers, attracted by 'the shrewdness of his remarks and general turn of conversation bestowed upon him their peculiar attention and favour'.[25]

His reputation as a local celebrity was now attracting attention from further afield. In June 1792, for example, the lively traveller Viscount John Byng, while staying at the Crown in Knaresborough, noted his disappointment at not meeting there one of the regulars – Blind Jack:

> I anxiously expected the company of (this inexplicable genius) John Metcalf who, for me, unluckily did not come home this night, but had gone to Spoffard (Spofforth). I should not have lost the sight of such a phenomenon – whom, they said, added to his other wonders the power of card-playing, and was a dab at put.[26]

Jack also visited relations and friends in Knaresborough, and was still being invited to play for entertainment and dances at the homes of gentlemen in the area. According to Thomas Sutcliffe, for example, the Revd Thomas Collins (the great-nephew of the first Revd Thomas Collins, who had died in 1788) told him that 'Jack had been accustomed to go regularly to play the fiddle' at his father's (James Collins's) house, i.e. Knaresborough House, near the site of his birthplace, now ironically playing for the family who had demolished his birthplace.[27]

At Christmas 1794, he paid a visit to the home of the late Colonel Thornton, the former captain, whose widow and son, Lieutenant-Colonel Thomas Thornton, remembered him well and were delighted to have him there to play his fiddle, something he had done so often before during the festive season:

> The reception he met with was such as fully reminded him of former days at Old Thornville, where he had spent many Christmases. The truly respectable Relict, and the worthy

Representative of his late Commander, always receive Blind Jack with a condescending affability, highly flattering to one in his humble station.[28]

As soon as Christmas was over he moved on to York, where he had not been for thirty-two years. He tapped his way round the old streets and snickleways that he once knew so well, pleased to note improvements that had been made in such streets as Spurriergate and the Pavement. His main reason for going back to York was to pay a visit to Middlethorpe, in order to renew his acquaintance with the Barlow family. His good friend Francis Barlow had died in 1771, but he was well known to his son, Samuel, the present squire, whose widow, incidentally, married Marcus Worsley of Hovingham Hall.[29, 30] As he made his way along the road to Bishopthorpe he realised that he had first followed this route sixty years before, when he had stayed with Squire Barlow for six months in 1735. As he approached the mansion he felt for a double gate in the wall, and noted that it had been hung in a different position from the one his sensitive memory so clearly recalled:

> At Mr Barlow's he stayed several nights which, he scarcely needs add, were spent most agreeably, he endeavouring to make his fiddle speak the satisfaction and hilarity felt by its owner.[31]

He says that he returned to York and spent several nights at the house of another friend, leaving on 10 January 1795. This is a significant date. Later that year he published the account of his life, dictated for the York booksellers and printers Edward & Robert Peck of Low Ousegate.[32] It seems clear, because he refers to no other visit to York, that during those few days in January he had a series of interviews with the printer and publisher. This is confirmed by a later edition of *The Life of John Metcalf*, published by Edward Peck in London in 1812. Here he describes himself as 'the original compiler', using italics, because by then the little book was appearing in pirated editions. He describes how some of Metcalf's friends in Harrogate had:

> …suggested to him the advantage of throwing together the leading incidents of his life, which he accordingly prepared to do, and principally with this view set out on foot to the city of York at the commencement of the year 1795 and the seventy-eighth year of his age.[33]

While he spent a few days at the house of a friend, he adds, 'the publisher compiled from his own narrative the particulars which constitute this story.'

During the same period the publishers arranged for his three-quarter length portrait to be drawn by J.R. Smith. Described by Hargrove, who knew him well, as 'an excellent likeness', this is the only known portrait of Blind Jack. All the rest are copies and variants of it, some of very poor draughtsmanship. The published version of this engraving – based on the only portrait of him from life – bears the caption, 'John Metcalf, aged seventy-eight'. This was the age he had just reached when the book was finally published, on 31 August 1795, later prints and editions adjusting the age.

It cannot have been a straightforward matter to write down John Metcalf's account of his life. Although he presumably showed his interviewer letters, or notes, such as accounts kept by Dolly of his income, he would very largely rely on his phenomenal memory and give a forthright and fluent narration. The problem, however, was twofold. First, he was rambling and discursive, rarely giving dates or a clear idea of the order of events. Secondly, he spoke not just with the strong North Riding accent of his Knaresborough upbringing, but in actual dialect, which meant that occasional vocabulary and idiomatic phrases would not be understood by the amanuensis and editor Edward Peck, who apologetically explained in the Preface:

> The person whose task it was to render it, in some degree, fit for the press, had much difficulty to encounter in arranging the dates, scarce any attention having been paid to chronological order; and the various anecdotes having been set down, as the recollection of them arose in the mind of the narrator, by an amanuensis wholly unqualified for the purpose, and given in a language intelligible to those only who are well acquainted with the Yorkshire dialect.[34]

This is followed by an admission that Metcalf's original first-person account has been changed to the third 'to avoid constantly recurring egotisms'. Then there is the important statement, that in spite of alterations and interlineations the account is substantially correct, having been read to Blind Jack for his approval.[35]

The last paragraph of the editorial is not at all convincing when it claims that Jack's original words are used in the snatches of dialogue. This is surely part of the spin designed to sell this account to the well-educated visitors to Harrogate:

> Though it was absolutely necessary to bring the style into something like grammatical order, and to purge it of barbarisms, yet pains have been taken to preserve its simplicity; and in some instances, where a few sentences of dialogue are introduced, the original words remain. Imperfect as it is, a hope is nevertheless entertained that it will prove amusing; and happy shall the Author of its Apology be, if the profits arising from the sale shall prove of sufficient value to smooth the decline of a life, which, though marked by eccentricity, has not been spent in vain.

Having finished his one literary piece of work Blind Jack set out from York on foot, walking the 10 miles to Old Thornville in three and a half hours. Here he spent the night, a tail piece to his visit of a couple of weeks earlier. The following morning he set out to walk to Knaresborough and apparently rounded off the Christmas season at Scriven Hall there, because he says he joined the birthday festivities of Sir Thomas Slingsby's eldest son, 'kept with the utmost festivity'.[36]

What he described as 'this imperfect sketch of a life' was published on the last day of August 1795, still in time to cash in on the season at Harrogate, where he went to sell copies to the spa visitors. A few would remember him from the old days, and many would know of his reputation as musician, horseman, gambler, lover and colourful character, to which was now added fame as a builder of roads. As he sat in the Queen's Head and the Royal Oak, selling his life story, we can be sure he would enhance it with lively oral additions, his commentary interspersed with drinking and card playing, with plenty of good company to cheer him in his eighties. Hargrove gave him extra publicity in the fifth edition of his *History* (1798), noting that Metcalf had published:

> …an account of his life and wonderful adventures, to which his portrait is fixed, and is a most excellent likeness. With this publication he daily attends the Spa season, and disposes of many copies to the visitors.[37]

The book sold well enough to go into a second edition in 1801 and a third in 1804, these printed by Edward Baines of Mercury Court, Leeds. In the second edition a new preface points out that Metcalf, now nearly eighty-four, still 'attends the Harrogate summer season', playing cards as well as his fiddle, but notes that he 'does not play for money, but for liquor or a little diversion'. The way Metcalf ends the new Preface shows how he was still enjoying, at the age of eighty-four, his role as a notable spa personality, yet habitually flattering and ingratiating himself with the wealthy visitors who, even now, could still provide him with income by buying his life story:

> Under these impressions, I beg leave humbly to offer to Your Patronage, this Second Edition of the *History* of some of the more striking incidents and adventures of my Life. And to assure you that words cannot express the pleasure and satisfaction I feel, in thus having an opportunity, before I am laid low, of declaring and subscribing myself, My Lords, Ladies, and Gentlemen, with profound esteem and heartfelt gratitude,
>
> > Your obliged, obedient,
> > > and humble servant,
> > > > John Metcalf,
> > > > > otherwise
> > > > > > Blind Jack.
> > > > > > > Spofforth, 29th July, 1801.[38]

As he moved through his eighties into his nineties, life in Spofforth, though much quieter than in Knaresborough and Harrogate, must have been very pleasant. An indication that he was by no means forgotten in his extreme age, but was still highly regarded, is that he was provided with three free dinners a week, paid for by the Earl of Egremont, who owned land locally and, as a descendant of the ancient Percy family, was patron of Spofforth church and a nobleman noted for philanthropy.[39] We owe the information about these years to Thomas Sutcliffe, who made a sketch of Blind Jack's home in Spofforth, showing the church behind it. He had been told this by a lady aged eighty-nine, who was the daughter of the landlord of the only inn in Spofforth in Blind Jack's time. There is a local tradition that this was the White Horse, and that Jack enjoyed playing cards and dominoes here.[40] The landlord's daughter said that the 'Arle o' Agrimony' (Lord Egremont) had ensured that Jack paid no rent and took his three meals a week at the inn.

This woman remembered this well because she usually served him the dinners herself and recalled that he would sometimes say to her, in a rare quotation of Blind Jack speaking in his usual North Riding dialect:

> Here, lass! Come an' 'ave a game wi' me – an' then thoo'll be able to say, when thoo's an auld woman, 'at thoo's played cards wi' Blind Jack.[41]

Though he continued to enjoy convivial drinking in the pubs, there is evidence that he also liked a nice cup of tea at his daughter's home, Blind Jack's handsome blue-patterned white teapot having been presented by a descendant to Knaresborough Town Council.[42]

Evidence that in retirement Blind Jack was a celebrity well known beyond the borders of Yorkshire is shown by the special visit paid to him on 7 May 1782 by James Plumptre (1770-1832), the clergyman-playwright of Norwich, a great traveller and connoisseur of late eighteenth-century England. The account of his visit to the man he describes as 'that extraordinary character... commonly called Blind Jack of Knaresborough' is valuable as an external source, confirming so much of what Metcalf, through his York publishers, tells us about himself.

Plumptre describes him as then aged eighty-two, 'above 6ft high, and of a very stout make'.

He then refers to his being blinded by smallpox, and the remarkable pursuits of his childhood and adolescence. 'Music he acquired, of course, but hunting, racing, horse-dealing, cock-fighting and card-playing, seem almost incredible.' He then refers to his elopment with Dolly, 'when he borrowed the eyes of a friend to assist him', his service with Colonel Thornton (as he then was) and his later work in making roads, bridges and houses. The account continues:

> He has walked several journeys to and from London, and never forgets a way he has once been. When I entered the room where he was sitting, and accosted him, he rose from his chair and said with a smile 'he never had the pleasure of seeing me before', for he distinguishes people by their voices as accurately as others do by the sight, and will recollect people he has heard but once at a great distance of time. I sat with him some time, and was much pleased with his placid and cheerful manner. There is a life of him published, but he told me many anecdotes of himself, which I have not noted among my memorandums, concluding I had them in the book, but they are not there, and I cannot now sufficiently depend upon my memory to relate them.[43]

How interesting it would have been if Plumptre had had the presence of mind to write down those unpublished anecdotes given to him by Blind Jack! At least he was the first to record something not prominent in the published memoirs – Jack's pride in his family. One thing Plumptre did bother to make a note of was the remarkable progeny which was a comfort to Blind Jack's old age: 'He has had 4 children, 19 grandchildren and 35 great- [and] great-great-grandchildren.'

The most important testimony of all recorded by Plumptre was a rare comment by Metcalf on his attitude to his blindness. Far from speaking with bitterness of all he had been denied, we find that he spoke of the advantages of his situation:

> He thought Providence knew what was best for us. His disposition was enterprising, and had his sight been spared it might have been worse for him.[44]

There is no hint of Blind Jack ever having been ill, but his exceptional health and strength finally gave way to inevitable mortality. We know nothing of how he died, but we can be sure he would have been ministered to by his daughter Ellen, and her family. His death took place on the 26 April 1810. He was ninety-two, a venerable patriarch, leaving behind a tribe of descendants – Plumptre's figure being brought up to date by Hargrove, no doubt with information from Metcalf families around Knaresborough, as 'four children, twenty grandchildren and ninety great- and great- great-grandchildren.'[45]

The funeral took place four days later at Spofforth parish church. The clerk was apparently moved to write just a little more in the parish register than the customary bare name, but all he managed was: '30th April, John Metcalf, a Blind Man'.[46]

His family alone would have ensured a crowded funeral service, his many descendants in attendance being a vivid reminder of his prodigious energy and enterprise. He was buried on the north side of the church, about halfway along, in a peaceful rural setting, still unchanged. A large headstone was provided by Lord Dundas of Kerse (1741-1820), a wealthy and philanthropic member of the Society of Antiquaries, and also – in his capacity as Commandant of the North York Militia – appreciative of Jack's service as a soldier.[47] The anonymous epitaph in verse, much superior to the lines on Dolly's headstone in Stockport, comes very close to doing Blind Jack justice:

Here lies John Metcalf, one whose infant sight

Felt the dark pressure of an endless night;
Yet such the fervour of his dauntless mind,
His limbs full strung, his spirits unconfin'd,
That long ere yet life's bolder years began,
His sightless efforts mark'd th' aspiring man,
Nor mark'd in vain – High deeds his manhood dar'd,
And commerce, travel, both his ardour shar'd;
'Twas his, a guide's unerring aid to lend;
O'er trackless wastes to bid new roads extend;
And when Rebellion rear'd her giant size,
'Twas his to burn with patriot enterprize –
For parting wife and babes one pang to feel,
Then welcome danger for his country's weal.
Reader! like him, exert thy utmost talent given;
Reader! like him, adore the bounteous hand of Heaven![48]

The headstone (below) is in good condition, little eroded. Not many pilgrims beat a path to see it, and sometimes, on my own visits, I have seen only sheep, which safely graze amongst the graves, keeping him company.

Blind Jack's grave is well worth a visit. It is a moving experience just to stand there and read the epitaph, and to think that in this earth there rests that giant frame, once animated by a powerful mind and spirit. Here lies all that was mortal of a unique and inspirational man, a classic legend in his lifetime, a man who refused to be beaten by any other obstacle than death itself.

Chapter Fourteen

Opinion and Evaluation

The news of Blind Jack's death was naturally the talk of Yorkshire, especially in Knaresborough and Harrogate, but it was also of sufficient national interest for an obituary to appear in the *Gentleman's Magazine* of 1810. This erroneously described him as having died 'aged ninety-four', but gave a column concisely summarising his life, clearly borrowed from Hargrove, who had in turn taken phrases from George Bew. There was no attempt to evaluate Metcalf's achievements, but at least this entry in a prestigious London journal showed that his fame had spread well beyond the north of England. Indeed, he had already been featured, three years earlier, in *The Eccentric Mirror* magazine, which asked nationwide readers the rhetorical question: 'Who would expect a man, totally blind from his infancy, superintending the building of bridges and the construction of highroads?'[1]

The following year Hargrove republished Peck's 1795 version of Blind Jack's autobiography, issuing it 'from Hargrove's Office, Knaresborough', and selling it in Knaresborough and Harrogate, and also in York at the bookshop of Wilson & Son. The appearance of posthumous editions like this, as we have noted, was what prompted Edward Peck to republish his own version in London in 1812. The text of all these early editions is identical, and the only kind of comment that Hargrove permits himself in this 1811 edition is that he opens with the phrase: 'This extraordinary character', which is no more than what he had already written in his *History of Knaresborough* (1809). He does, however, take the opportunity to correct his mistake made in both this and earlier editions of this book, in which he had carelessly assumed the age Jack started school (four) was the age he contracted smallpox.[2]

The following year, in 1812, there appeared a new edition of the *Life*, presumably not authorised by Edward Peck, printed and published by James Kendrew of Colliergate, York, who had earlier cashed in on Knaresborough's historical characters by publishing an account of the trial of Eugene Aram. Kendrew's edition is a faithful reproduction of Peck, but he adds a curious moralising conclusion in verse, perhaps written by himself. In this he does not so much extol Blind Jack's virtues as express the view that (rather as Beethoven had said 'I shall hear in heaven!') there would be compensation for Jack and all others like him in the light perpetual that lies beyond death:

Now if soldier or statesman of whatever age or nation,
He hereafter may be, should hear this relation,
And of eyesight bereft should like him grope his way,
The bright sunbeams of virtue will turn night into day;
So he to distress and darkness inur'd,
In his vile crust of clay when no longer immured,
At death's welcome stroke his bright course would begin
And enjoy endless day from the sunshine within.[3]

Kendrew went on to produce seven editions, many selling in London. Most of these reprints of Peck lacked any commentary, either in verse or prose. Soon after Blind Jack's death the standard life appeared in Johnson's *Penny Library*, a cheap series of booklets which included accounts ranging from John Wesley to Maria Marten and the Murders in the Red Barn. The subtitle of the Metcalf story enticed prospective readers with the promise of 'an amusing account of his elopement and marriage to Miss Benson, and details of his Career as a Soldier' – these last words in block letters. It did however conclude what was really presented just as an entertaining tale with the serious observation that though Blind Jack had spent eighty-seven of his years 'in perpetual darkness… the Almighty had endowed him with abilities to undertake and complete a number of contracts, not inferior to many experienced ingineers'.[4]

The fact that memories of Blind Jack were very much alive in the Harrogate area is shown by the attempted witticism of Dr Adam Hunter, a physician writing in 1830, pointing out that in recent years there had been improved access to the spa:

> …though there is still room left for additional amendment; nor is this to be wondered at seeing that a blind man was in the first instance employed to lay out the principal lines of road in the neighbourhood, upon the ingenious principle, doubtless, that where such an individual could travel, any one with two eyes might surely follow.[5]

In his footnote about Blind Jack he unfortunately fails to mention his direct contribution to the prosperity of the spa, namely his many years there as the principal musician.

Familiarity with his road-making accomplishments was by this time nationwide and also becoming known in America, as is indicated by *Biography of the Blind*, the book first published in 1821 by James Wilson, himself blind from infancy. The chapter on John Metcalf was simply an edited version of Peck, with additions from Bew. It gave no new information, but at least it was recognition, helping to give credit to Blind Jack well beyond the boundaries of Yorkshire – a story, says Wilson, which 'cannot fail to excite no small degree of astonishment and admiration.'[6]

As well as being of great interest to those concerned with the blind, this outstanding Yorkshire character was of special interest to those interested in civil engineering and the history of the Industrial Revolution. The first and most important of these was Samuel Smiles, who devoted a good number of pages to 'John Metcalf, Road-Maker' in his *Lives of the Engineers* (1861), more or less repeated in his *Life of Telford* (1867) and *The History of Roads* (1878). Smiles gave the world, for the first time, a balanced account of Blind Jack, including the anecdotal material from Knaresborough we have previously referred to, and also gave his opinion of the importance and achievement of this 'strong-hearted and resolute man', who 'not only made the highways which were designed for him, but himself personally surveyed and laid out many of the important roads which he constructed in difficult and mountainous parts of Yorkshire and Lancashire.'[7]

Smiles presented John Metcalf to the world as 'the first great English road-maker.'[8] He saw him as a precursor of Telford and McAdam, and also of George Stephenson, who had followed him in using the same method for carrying his railway over Chat Moss (between Manchester and Liverpool) as Jack had used to carry his roads over Yorkshire marshes:

> It consisted simply in a large extension of the bearing surface, by which, in fact, the road was made to float upon the surface of the bog. And the ingenuity of the expedient proved the practical shrewdness and mother-wit of the blind Metcalf, as it afterwards illustrated the promptitude, as well as the skill, of the clear-sighted George Stephenson.[9]

Around the time of the Samuel Smiles publications, a Victorian local historian who was an early authority on Harrogate, William Grainge, showed his appreciation of Blind Jack by including him in his booklet *Three Wonderful Yorkshire Characters* (1864), the other two being Henry Jenkins, indisputably Yorkshire's oldest man, who died in 1670 supposedly aged 169, and Peg Wharton, a wealthy eighteenth-century eccentric, who died at the age of 122. Though Blind Jack, with his mere ninety-two years, managed less longevity than the other two, his story is far more soundly based on historical evidence, as is clear from the brief account Grainge gives of the life of 'the self-taught Engineer', of whom he makes the succinct assessment:

> One of the most remarkable instances on record of the difficulties of blindness and want of education being overcome by perseverance and industry.[10]

Grainge was so interested in the subject of long life that earlier the same year he had published his *Yorkshire Longevity*, in which he included, in his alphabetical list of long-living Yorkshire people, the same piece on Blind Jack.[11] Grainge's account of Blind Jack appeared for a third time in 1881, in *Old Yorkshire*.[12]

A more influential Victorian author than Grainge was the antiquarian vicar of Horbury Bridge, near Wakefield, the Revd Sabine Baring-Gould, best known for the hymn 'Onward, Christian Soldiers!' He was a prolific writer of prose, including *Yorkshire Oddities, Incidents and Strange Events* (1874), among whose thirty or so characters is Blind Jack. His chapter on him is simply a retelling of the story which, he says, he has found in the chapbook from Johnson's *Penny Library*. However, he introduces it as a Devon man who has lived both in the West and East Ridings, and has learnt to admire the drive and determination of Yorkshire folk:

> Blind Jack Metcalf is certainly one of the most remarkable characters that Yorkshire has produced. Afflicted with loss of sight, the indomitable energy of his true north-country character enabled him to carry on a successful business where many a south countryman would have failed.[13]

It is noticeable, incidentally, that the clergyman author carefully leaves out certain unedifying aspects of Blind Jack's life, in particular all mention of his affair with the Knaresborough woman who bore his child.

The contribution of John Metcalf continued to be mentioned, though not in any detail, by writers on the history of transport, as in, for example, Mark Searle's large illustrated volume, *Turnpikes and Tollbars* (1920), where he comments, comparing him with the famous successor to Newton, that Blind Jack 'far surpasses all that has been recorded of Professor Saunderson… and other remarkable persons of that unfortunate class.'[14]

In the early part of the twentieth century, interest in Blind Jack was enthusiastically revived by Halifax-born J.S. Fletcher, the popular writer of crime fiction who was also a serious historian of Yorkshire and a Fellow of the Royal Historical Society. In 1900 he first drew attention to Metcalf in his monumental six-volume *A Picturesque History of Yorkshire*, though briefly, with the apology that 'of the life history of this truly remarkable person, to whom the loss of sight seems to have meant nothing, it is impossible to speak properly within circumscribed limits.'[15] Fletcher made the most of further opportunities to express his admiration of Blind Jack. For example, a few years later he wrote of him in *The Enchanting North*:

…one of the most striking examples of what human fortitude, resolution and patience can do in face of adverse circumstances. He lost his sight at the age of six, yet at the end of a very long life could truthfully say that he knew his way about his native county far better than most people whose eyesight was unimpaired.[16]

Ten years later Fletcher returned to Blind Jack in his perceptively analytical book, *The Making of Modern Yorkshire*, published in 1918. In this he opens his second chapter, 'Communication and Transit', with a description of work on the Ferrensby-Minskip Turnpike. He sets the scene with his skill as a writer of fiction: the gangs of labourers armed with their picks and shovels, the cottages requisitioned for their accommodation, the horses and carts bringing the gravel – the whole energised by this 'tall broad-shouldered man', arriving at first light, briskly tapping his way with a long staff, carrying on his shoulders a great load of meat for his men. Before going on to give an account of Blind Jack's life, and especially his contribution to the development of Yorkshire's turnpike trust network in the second half of the eighteenth century, he lavishes praise on him in a way that had never been done before:

He is certainly entitled to rank with the greatest of his fellow countrymen. No Yorkshireman has ever shown more of that peculiar spirit of grit which is the Yorkshireman's finest quality. Nowhere in the whole history of mankind is there a finer record of moral bravery than his… In his manifestation of certain qualities he towered above all his fellows.[17]

A couple of years later Fletcher published his *Story of English Towns*, and in the pages on Knaresborough he naturally referred to Blind Jack again, describing him as 'one of the greatest of all Yorkshiremen, a shining example of the way in which men can rise superior to one of the heaviest of human afflictions.'[18]

It is easy to gain the impression from champions of Blind Jack such as J.S. Fletcher that he was the only road-maker of his day. He was, of course, one of a number. But he was certainly one of the very best, constantly being offered work by the turnpike trusts. It was not just the novelty of his being blind that attracted attention, but the quality and originality of his work.

No doubt influenced by J.S. Fletcher, always readable and scholarly, various subsequent writers on Yorkshire have given due attention to Blind Jack. We find it, for example, in G.C. Heseltine's *Great Yorkshiremen* (1932), Lettice Cooper's *Great Men* (1955), Marie Hartley and Joan Ingilby's *Yorkshire Portraits* (1961) and Harry J. Scott's *Yorkshire Heritage* (1970).

In Knaresborough itself there has always been a feeling of pride in Blind Jack, with numerous reprints of the slightly extended 1795 *Life*, originally printed here by Hargrove, followed by William Langdale and William Parr. From 1977 the Courthouse Museum has displayed a life-size effigy of Jack standing with his original oaken staff and viameter. In the Market Place he is commemorated by Blind Jack's pub (which I was invited to open in 1991). In 2005 it was proposed to erect a bronze statue, and the following year two small maquettes were displayed in Knaresborough Library so the public could vote for their preference. One, by Ian Judd, showed Blind Jack on the road, wheeling his viameter. The other, by Barbara Asquith, showed him sitting on a seat, holding his viameter. My choice would certainly have been the first, because it gave a characteristic glimpse of Blind Jack standing tall, a man of action. By a narrow margin, however, the voting was in favour of the seated statue, and people liked the idea of having their photo taken sitting next to him.

Reference has already been made to a number of books specifically concerned with the history of roads and transport, and in many general history books Blind Jack has at least a mention. Typically he is seen as a precursor of other famous road-makers, as in the comment: 'The work of Metcalf, and later of Macadam and Telford, made possible the era of the stage-coach.'[19] And writers on the history of road-making have no hesitation in describing Metcalf as 'a gifted surveyor'.[20] Similar recognition is given in more recent publications such as *The Biographical Dictionary of Civil Engineers: 1500-1830*, (2002)[21] and the *Oxford Dictionary of National Biography*, (2004).[22]

In Alan White's novel, *The Years of Change* (1983), Blind Jack is briefly depicted taking on men to work on his roads, and never making a mistake because 'he can tell a man's character from his voice'. An account of him is given by two men he employs. They are impressed by the uncanny knowledge he has of the terrain, the way he gets them to break up stones to the required size, then uses them to fill in any depression made the first time the heavy vehicles are driven over the new surface. There is trouble from an anti-turnpike mob, stirred up by wagoners who resent paying extra tolls. They set fire to a toll house and attack the two men, Copley and Aysgill, who are central to the story. When Blind Jack arrives with the rest of his men, he fires his 'brace of pistols' and drives off the mob, but not before they have killed Copley.[23] Though such attacks were not uncommon, if Metcalf had been involved in something of this kind we can be sure he would have made the most of it in his memoirs.

In my own presentations of Blind Jack I have tried to keep to the historical facts, filling these out with local colour and dialect. The first of these was when I narrated a dramatised account on Radio Leeds in 1971, using a young man born and bred in Knaresborough to play the part of Jack, and providing atmosphere with fiddle music of the period and sounds of hammering and ramming down stones on the road. In 1972 we included Blind Jack in the Castle Pageant, using Knaresborough Castle as the stage. Up there on the ramparts I interviewed the old road-maker as he demonstrated the use of his original viameter, borrowed from the nearby Courthouse Museum. This Blind Jack was played by an elderly man of similar build and style, with a deep, booming voice and an authentic Yorkshire accent. Arthur Mann really brought Blind Jack to life again, with his commanding presence and comments such as: 'Ee! She wor a grand woman, wor Dolly!'

In later performances of this historical pageant another effective John Metcalf was Phil Brown, and in the most recent version of his resurrection (in the Millennium Pageant which I presented at Knaresborough Castle in June 2000) he was played by another local man of exactly the right build and speech, Derek Van Zelst. So in this way we materialised four different Blind Jacks, each with his own special contribution. Most recently, just before this book was completed, it was a privilege to give one of my talks on Blind Jack, illustrated by artifacts and his kind of music, in the assembly room of Knaresborough House, within a stone's throw of his birthplace, and in the very room once enlivened by the sound of his violin.

What, then, after all these years of thinking about this phenomenal man, is my own considered opinion of him? In the first place, he *was* a phenomenon, absolutely outstanding, unique as a blind road builder, memorable for his charismatic drive and versatile accomplishment. But this gives rise to the question that is most frequently asked, and it is essential that we return to this before we go any further. The fact that John Metcalf did so much, so well, over such a long lifetime, makes us ask the fundamental question: 'Was he really blind?' That is, in the sense that he was totally blind, what his contempories called 'blind as a stone'.

I believe that he was, for the following reasons. First of all, the foul disease of smallpox really was capable of damaging the cornea to such an extent that nothing could be seen, not even a remnant of peripheral vision – except that, as was said earlier, it just might be possible to distinguish between brilliant sunlight and total darkness. There are plenty of well-documented statistics to show that smallpox was a common cause of complete blindness, especially in infancy and early childhood.

Secondly, there is a long succession of witnesses who must have been able to tell whether he was blind or not. We are not dealing with a few isolated anecdotes about a man supposed to be blind. He was fully integrated into society, and such as the following persons would have been in prolonged or frequent contact with him, noticing how he behaved, usually at close quarters. There were, for example, family and friends, visitors to the spa, gentlemen and their ladies, a number of whom invited him to play at their country houses. In particular, he would have been closely observed by such experienced men as Francis Barlow, George Grey and Colonel Liddell. There were his fellow musicians and his fellow soldiers in the Yorkshire Blues, as well as Captain Thornton, and even the Duke of Cumberland. Then, of course, there were his many contacts in different parts of Yorkshire and the North, and in London. In addition, he worked closely with the officers of various turnpike trusts and the hundreds of men who worked for him on the roads, and others with whom he arranged contracts.

Then we have those who specifically interviewed him, such as George Bew, James Plumptre and Edward Peck. The point is that from all those who knew him, over all those years, there has not been a single suggestion that any contemporary questioned his blindness. The people who were in a position to judge accepted him as genuinely and totally blind, and I believe we must leave it at that.

Assuming, then, that he was indeed blind, the next obvious question is: did he really do all that he claimed to do? It is one thing to say that a blind person makes remarkable compensatory adjustments and manages a virtually normal life. But in the case of Blind Jack the range and standard of his accomplishments would be absolutely outstanding for any sighted person. So the sceptics – if they cannot challenge his blindness – challenge his truthfulness, and say that he could not possibly have done all he claimed to do.

Once again, it is a question of whether or not we are willing to accept the testimony of his contemporaries. The very people who took it for granted that he was blind were the ones who were amazed at what they saw him do. It is true that most of his story is what he tells us himself, as a man proud of his achievements. But not only are there many little external pieces of evidence which help to confirm the personal narrative, the fact is that his life story was not just a boastful piece of self publishing, but something he was encouraged to do by his friends and by two reputable printers and publishers.

Moreover, as his story first appeared in print in 1795, that left fifteen years while he was still alive, during which his claims could have been challenged and contradicted – particularly by the various important local gentlemen and their families whose names he mentions. Yet, the 1795 publication went into several different prints and editions during his lifetime without a single alteration being made to his story.

This does not, of course, mean that we must take everything that Metcalf tells us at face value. Those of us who are old enough know that we can remember with wonderful clarity something that happened to us fifty, sixty, seventy years ago, especially if it was something unusual and dramatic. But we also know that memory can play us tricks, and when we compare our version of a particular incident with that of someone who also experienced it, we sometimes find we have misremembered and that details are omitted, or exaggerated. So, no doubt, in the case of Blind Jack – though, as he pointed out to George Bew, it was the very fact that he could not see that made him commit everything so carefully and systematically to his memory.[24]

Knaresborough House today.

In discussing the astonishing catalogue of events which Blind Jack presents us with, I have sometimes met people who take the view that he was a plausible Munchausen-style leg-puller. These claims could not possibly be true, they say. But we are not dealing here with some apocryphal tale, put into print long years after the alleged events, as in the case of Robin Hood or Mother Shipton. This was a story by a person who was still alive, with a number of those who feature in the story still alive – or at least within living memory.

What is more, though by no means everything can be confirmed by primary historical sources, sufficient of Blind Jack's statements about his roads have documentary evidence to support them. If we can show that he was telling the truth about his most famous and, indeed, spectacular achievements, why should we be so sceptical about the rest?

It must, of course, be conceded that we cannot rule out the possibility of colourful exaggeration, as well as the distortions and misunderstandings of an amanuensis who admitted he had difficulty in understanding Blind Jack. But the manuscript of 1795, we are plainly told, had been read over to Metcalf so that he could make any corrections he desired. So what he tells, together with the evidence of others, seems to me to be pretty convincing. It all fits so neatly into the historical context. And my position is simply this: it is extraordinary. It is astounding. But it has the ring of truth.

The nearest we come to Metcalf's own explanation of his ability is in what he told George Bew – the emphasis on meticulous memorising that we have already noted. Perhaps because he had started his life of blindness, at the age of six, with some vivid visual memories, he had found a way of mapping out in his mind the surroundings he could not see, always retaining a sense of spatial awareness. Allied to this was his use of what is now called 'echolocation', which is 'seeing with sound', a kind of sonar. He learnt to develop acutely sensitive hearing which could tell him – by the sound of his tapping stick and cautious footsteps – exactly where he was. He also had the assistance of other people and of his horses and dogs – both of these serving the function of the now familiar 'guide dogs for the blind'. The long horseback journeys he made in Yorkshire, and even up to Scotland, become credible if we accept with Samuel Smiles that 'he trusted much, no doubt, to the sagacity of his horse.'

As he told James Plumptre, he identified people by their distinctively individual voices, but even when they did not speak he could sense their presence. This is shown by an anecdote preserved by the Victorian visitor to Knaresborough, Thomas Sutcliffe. He says that a newly married woman was standing at her door when she noticed Blind Jack coming up the street. Knowing that he always recognised people by their voices, she did not speak, and kept perfectly still. As soon as he drew near he said: 'Good morning, Mrs Thornton'. As she had only been married a few days the woman was amazed, but it was assumed that he had heard where she was living and knew when he had reached the house. He got into conversation with her, and later met her husband, accosting him with the words: 'Y've lit of a squary neece woman for a wife, Thornton!'[25]

This little story illustrates that Jack coped with his blindness essentially by not allowing himself to become isolated from society. From the very beginning he was always involved – with boys of his own age, with dogs and horses, with his music, but especially with people. Few disabled by blindness can have been more gregarious, and it was his habitual contact with sighted folk in everyday life that helped to sharpen his perceptiveness.

Nevertheless, although gregarious and extroverted, happiest when with other people, especially Dolly and his children, and with animals, Blind Jack could also enjoy the inner world of his mind. If not filled with images we can be sure it would be filled with music – and with mathematical concepts. This is something he had in common – to a tiny extent – with Nicholas Saunderson. It is clear that Metcalf had real facility in mental arithmetic and the calculations required in quantity surveying – something which must have been of great benefit to him in a road-making career.

He had an acute interest in financial matters, and like a good Yorkshireman, was canny with his brass. He loved to strike a good bargain, and was adept at the sharp deal known as 'the Yorkshire bite', forever stating prices and profits and loss. He even retained the figures – perhaps with some written record he had kept – of all he received for his road-making. Edward Peck, who carefully discussed this with him, said the total of his contracts was 'the astonishing sum of fifty-five thousand pounds and upwards, which… would infer a prodigious spirit of industry and talent.'[26] Other estimates of income have been higher, and Smiles, for example, gives his income for 'about 180 miles' of road as £65,000 – though once again it must be stressed that this sum was the total of what he was paid by the turnpike trusts and not his profit.[27]

His contribution as a road builder is, of course, his essential claim to fame – and his place in the history of civil engineering beyond dispute. And it must be repeated that it is not just a matter of the novelty of his achievements in spite of blindness. He was a fine musician in his own right. He was an accomplished road builder in his own right – a recognised pioneer, who always worked to a high standard and completed his contracts on or before time.

Though John Loudon McAdam (who was wealthy and influential, working at national level) revolutionised road-making by binding the surface with coal-tar to form the now universally-adopted tarmac, his basic design of graded stones and cambered, well-drained roads, had been anticipated by Blind Jack some seventy years earlier. When we ride over certain of our modern roads today it is good to remember that we are following a course laid out by an eighteenth-century contractor and his men, their original work forever concealed by the modern tarmac.

Those who have heard of Blind Jack tend to think of him exclusively as a road builder. But it must be remembered that he also made a name for himself as a musician, and that on all

Trompe l'oeil window, Blind Jack's pub. (Peter Kearney)

his travels he was never without his violin and oboe. In his introduction to Samuel Howell's *Fourteen Lithographic Views of Knaresborough* (1838), Dr J. Doran notes the tradition that Blind Jack 'played on the fiddle like an angel'. And the quality of his musicianship is surely indicated by the fact that he was not only a popular spa musician, but always sure of a welcome as a player at prestigious country houses to the end of his long life – to say nothing of his having served as a military musician, and being chosen to play by the Duke of Cumberland.

The principal explanation of how John Metcalf was able to do what he did leads us to a discussion of his character. He was, to say the least, a very determined man, with a single-minded drive to dominate his circumstances, one that had characterised him from early childhood. He simply would not be beaten. It was as though, even as a little boy, he had reacted as defiantly as Beethoven when devastated by his deafness, and cried out with him: 'I will take Fate by the throat! It shall not wholly overcome me.'

This resolve to tackle all the problems that beset him, this energetic drive that carried him through the most daunting twists and turns of life, would not have meant much without his accompanying intelligence. There is no doubt that he was a clever and resourceful man, always eager to make an ingenious adaptation, the best example of this being his elopement and midnight marriage to Dolly.

Not only was Blind Jack quick-witted, he was a fluent conversationalist, with a ready repartee, and we have sufficient of Blind Jack's quips and comments to let us see how he handled himself. A good example of this is when he deftly parries the sarcastic remarks of the officers in Edinburgh, the episode concluding with the words:

Then, making his obeisance, he withdrew. For Metcalf, though he had not read books, had read men, and received his knowledge from the school of the world.[28]

Early commentators were impressed with the way in which a blind man with so little formal education was able to engage in buying and selling and all the transactions involved in making roads. Most impressive of all is the way Blind Jack was equally at ease whether dealing with the working class, his fellow musicians, ladies and gentlemen of the spa, the landed gentry, the racing fraternity, officers in the army, traders, turnpike trustees, hard-headed businessmen and ministers – though it must be said that he was always happier with publicans than with parsons.

Typical of the eighteenth century, he was a universal man with wide interests. To say he was a 'Jack of all trades' may seem appropriate, but the phrase implies a certain amateurishness – and whatever Blind Jack turned his hand to, he did it to a high standard. There is no denying that he was proud of his versatile and adventurous life and wanted the world to know about it. But he had a right to put on record what he had made out of such an adverse and unpromising beginning.

And his pride was counterbalanced by a certain humility – the way he acknowledged his indebtedness to Dolly and his patrons, and the several references to the way 'the hand of Providence' – a common eighteenth-century synonym for God – had supported and guided him through all his dangers and difficulties.[29] A widower for thirty-two years, he ended his days serene and cheerful, as Plumptre observed, with no bitterness about his blindness, because 'he thought Providence knew which was best for him'. That he was, for all his roguery, not an irreligious man is clearly implied in the concluding line of his epitaph, which exhorts the reader, ' like him', to 'adore the bounteous hand of Heaven.'

Providence had certainly blessed him with exceptionally good health. It is as though the virulent forces of disease, having failed to destroy him through smallpox at the age of six, had retreated in disgrace, never to touch him again. Those who knew him well, Edward Peck, for example, testified that 'the muscular powers of his strong frame yet remained unimpaired, and his spirits at eighty were as gay as a youth of eighteen.'[30]

It was this animation by a youthful spirit that struck people most. Peck put his finger on this feature of his personality when he noted that in the prime of life Jack possessed 'a peculiar archness of disposition, with an unceasing flow of spirit, and a contempt of danger.'[31] Today we hardly ever hear anyone described as 'arch', but it was once commonly used to mean 'playful', 'teasing', with an air of mischief making.

This was surely true of Blind Jack. He liked a joke, liked a drink, enjoyed more than the occasional flutter. He had also sown his wild oats, fathered a child he never supported, and eloped with his girl on the eve of her intended marriage to a rival. But there was a more serious side to his personality – his professional musicianship, his loyalty to his wife and children, his patriotic service as a soldier, his originality and reliability as a road-maker.

Above all, Blind Jack excels as an example of courageous determination to master the problems that confront us. He is a particular inspiration to those who are blind – as he was to the late Dr Kenneth Jernigan, famous president of the American organisation the National Federation of the Blind, who wrote in 1973, when describing the way in which blind people can overcome their difficulties: 'No-one has ever proved the point or showed the way with more flair than a stalwart Englishman of the eighteenth century named John Metcalf. Indeed, this brash fellow not only defied convention, but the world.'[32]

He may not have anything like the global recognition of such towering figures as Louis Braille or Helen Keller, but Blind Jack – with all his faults and eccentricities – is one of the great men of Yorkshire, of England – and, I would even say, of the whole of humanity.

Notes

Unless otherwise stated, the version of Blind Jack's memoirs referred to is the second edition (1801), printed by Edward Baines, Leeds.

Chapter 1

1. *The Life of John Metcalf, commonly called Blind Jack of Knaresborough* (1795), p. 1.
2. E. Hargrove, *The History of the Town, Castle and Forest of Knaresborough*, 6th edition (1809), p. 56.
3. B. Jennings, ed., *A History of Harrogate and Knaresborough* (1970), p. 209.
4. Hargrove, op. cit., p. 53.
5. *The Life of John Metcalf* (2nd edition) (1801), Dedication, p. iii.
6. S. Smiles, *Lives of the Engineers* (1861), Vol. 1, p. 210.
7. F. Collins, *The Family of Collins*, Knaresborough (1912), pp. 2-3.
8. Smiles, p. 209.
9. H. Speight, *Upper Nidderdale* (1906), p. 47, p. 49.
10. *Life* (note 5), p. 10.
11. Hargrove, *History of Knaresborough*, (4th edition) (1789), p. 64, (6th edition) (1809), p. 104.
12. G. Bew, *Memoirs of the Manchester Literary and Philosophical Society* (1782), Vol. 1, p. 172.
13. *York Courant*, 12 March 1745.
14. Voltaire, *Lettres sur les Anglais* (1734), ed. A. Wilson Green (1961), pp. 37-8, Note p. 139.
15. M. Neesam, *Harrogate Great Chronicle* (2005), pp. 97-100.
16. J. Wesley, *Primitive Physic* (1747), p. 58.
17. For a modern account of viral and bacterial damage to the cornea see, for example, *Professional Guide to Disease* (7th edition) (2001), p. 1188.
18. *Life* (1801), p. 10.
19. Ibid., p. 29.
20. Ibid., p. 10.
21. Ibid., pp. 10-11.

Chapter 2

1. Latin inscription recorded by W. Grainge, *A Historical and Descriptive Account of Knaresborough*, (1865), p. 73.
2. *Life* (1801), p. 11.
3. *The Family of Collins* (p. 2)
4. *Life*, p. 11.
5. Ibid., p. 13.
6. Ibid., pp. 13-14.
7. The Revd Dr James Talbot had been Rector of Spofforth from 1700 to 1708.
8. *Life*, pp. 14-15. It is stated here that the vicar was the Revd Mr Collins, but as he did not take over until 1735, when Jack was eighteen, this is a mistake. The incident obviously refers to the early teenage years
9. Ibid., p. 44.
10. *Life*, p. 15.
11. This inn was later called the George, then the Moray Arms, now the Yorkshire Lass.
12. *Life*, pp. 17-18.
13. Ibid., p. 18.

14. Ibid., p. 19.
15. Ibid., p. 20.
16. Ibid., p. 21.
17. Ibid., p. 22.
18. M.G. Neesam, *Harrogate Great Chronicle* (2005), p. 102.
19. G.A. Patmore, *An Atlas of Harrogate* (1963), p. 13.
20. D. Defoe, *A Tour Through England and Wales* (Everyman, 1928),Vol. 2., p. 213.
21. B. Jennings, ed., p.173.

Chapter 3

1. *The Diary of Sir Henry Slingsby,* ed. D. Parsons (1836), p. 330.
2. Hargrove (1789), p. 98.
3. T. Smollet, *The Expedition of Humphry Clinker* (1771), Oxford University Press World Classics, p. 195.
4. Ibid., p. 198.
5. Hargrove (1775), p. 54.
6. *The Life and Opinions of John Buncle, Esquire*, ed. E.A. Baker (1904), p. 285.
7. I.E. Broadhead, *Exploring Harrogate* (1984), p. 32.
8. *Life* (1801), p. 22.
9. Ibid, p. vi.
10. Ibid, p. 24.
11. Ibid, pp. 22-3.
12. D. Griffiths, *A Musical Place of the First Quality* (1994), p. 105, p. 108.
13. *Life* p. 24.
14. G. Worsley, 'Middlethorpe Hall', *Country Life*, (12 December 1985). Middlethorpe Hall brochure (2000), p. 2.
15. *Life*, p. 25.
16. Ibid., pp.18-30. The simile 'blind as a stone' was typical of the period, appearing as 'stone blind', for example, in Tristram Shandy (1759).
17. Ibid., p. 32.
18. Ibid., pp. 33-4.
19. Ibid., p. 36.
20. Hargrove (1809), p.123.
21. *Life*, pp. 36-37.
22. Ibid., p. 37.
23. W. Grainge, 'Yorkshire's Eccentric Characters,' *Old Yorkshire* (1883), ed. W. Smith,Vol. IV, p. 174.
24. *Life*, p. 38. This circular race was reconstructed on BBC TV by Adam Hart Davis in *Local Heroes* in 1992.
25. Ibid., pp. 38-39.

Chapter 4

1. *Life*, p. 34.
2. Ibid., pp. 34-36.
3. Ibid., pp. 48-49.
4. The Toy Shop is included in the view of Church Square (1833) ascribed to W.P. Frith. See Neesam, p. 106.
5. *Life*, pp. 39-42.
6. Ibid., p. 43.
7. Ibid., p. 44.

8. Ibid, p. 47.
9. The later term is 'affiliation'. An 'affiliation order' meant that the man judged to be the father of an illegitimate child is required to help to support it.
10. *Life*, pp. 50-51.
11. This was probably John Knowles of Plumpton, who lived to the age of ninety, died in 1791, and whose grave is in the Quaker burial ground at Scotton.
12. *Life*, pp. 51-2.
13. J. Wesley, *Journal*, 21 March 1770.
14. G. Tonstall, *A New Year's Gift for Doctor Witty* (1672), pp. 55-6.
15. *Life*, p. 53.
16. A Whitworth, *A to Z of Whitby History* (2002), pp. 9-10.
17. R. Welford, *Men of Note twixt Tyne and Tweed* (1895) Vol II, p. 353.
18. *Life*, p. 54. 'grogram' is a fairly coarse cloth made from silk combined with mohair or wool.
19. 'Flip', a mixture of beer, spirits and sugar usually mulled; 'bumbo', a mixture of rum and sugar, flavoured with nutmeg.
20. Situated on the southern side of the A64 near the junction for Flaxton.
21. *Life*, p. 57.

Chapter 5

1. *Life*, pp. 57-8.
2. R. Palmer, ed., *The Oxford Book of Sea Songs* (1986), pp. 126-9.
3. See G. Hogg, p. 52, A. Plowright, p. 244.
4. Smollett, op. cit., p. 197.
5. E. Pawson, *Transport and Economy* (1977), p. 268.
6. *Life*, p. 58.
7. Berwick History Society, *Berwick in Parliament* (2001), pp. 70-71.
8. *Life*., p. 59.
9. The amanuensis had written 'Welling'.
10. See p. 25.
11. *Life*, p. 60.
12. Hargrove (1775), pp. 54-55.
13. M. Colbeck, *Queer Folk* (1977), p. 85.
14. Smiles, p. 214.
15. *Life*, p. 61.
16. Ibid., pp. 61-2.
17. Ibid., p. 62.
18. Ibid., pp 62-3.
19. Ibid., 63.
20. Ibid., p. 64-5.
21. Neesam, p. 103, pp. 106-7.
22. Hogg, pp. 67-8, Plowright, p. 375.
23. *Life*, p. 66-7.

Chapter 6

1. *Life*, p. 69.
2. Ibid., p. 70.
3. Ibid., p. 71.
4. M. Neesam, *The Harrogate Great Chronicle* (2005), p. 313.
5. The author has been kindly shown around by the owner, J. Houston.

6. *Life*, p. 72.
7. Hogg, op.cit., p. 74.
8. Knaresborough Parish Register, North Yorkshire County Records Office, Northallerton.
9. *Life*, p. 73.
10. William Thornton's home, Thornville, at Cattal Magna, nearly 8 miles east of Knaresborough, is a fine Georgian house which can still be seen.
11 *Life*, p. 73.
12. Ibid., p. 74.
13. Ibid., p. 75.

Chapter 7

1. 'City of York House Book' (1747), B43, p. 249. York City Archives,
2. *York Courant*, 12 March 1744/5. (N.B. The year changed at the end of March.)
3. *The Gentleman's Magazine* (1758), p. 538.
4. H. Speight, *Nidderdale* (1894), p. 161.
5. *Life* p. 77.
6. J.R. Western, *The English Militia in the Eighteenth Century* (1965), pp.106-8.
7. *Life*, p. 78.
8. Ibid., pp. 79-80.
9. Ibid., p. 79.
10. W.A. Barrett, ed., *English Folk Songs*, n.d., p. 61.
11. *Life.*, p. 80.
12. *The London Evening Post*, 26-9 October 1745.
13. *Life*, p. 81.
14. The Blackett family was also associated with Newby Hall, where Blind Jack played (See *Life*, p. 22)
15. *Life*, pp. 82-3.

Chapter 8

1. *Life*, p. 86.
2. 'Matrosses', a term then used for assistant gunners, related to German *Matrose* (sailor).
3. P. Harrington, *Culloden* (1991), pp.18-19.
4. *Life*, p. 86.
5. Ibid., p. 87.
6. Harrington, pp.18, 20.
7. *Life*, pp. 89-91.
8. Ibid., pp. 92-93.
9. See Harrington, p. 17.
10. *Life*, p. 96.
11. Pladdie (tartan shawl, worn over the shoulder), brogues (rough shoes of leather).
12. Bannock (round, flat loaf, usually unleavened), mutchkin (measure equivalent to about three-quarters of a pint, wame (stomach).
13. *Life*, p. 98.
14. Ibid., p. 95.
15. Ibid., p. 99.
16. Ibid., p. 101.
17. J. Oates, 'Independent Volunteer Forces in Yorkshire', *Yorkshire Archaeological Journal,* Vol. 73, p.129.

Chapter 9

1. J. Prebble, *Culloden* (1961), p. 100, *Life*, p. 102.
2. *Life*, p. 103.
3. See, for example, Harrington, p. 44, c.f. *Life*, p. 104.
4. *Life*, p. 103. The amanuensis wrote 'Thornton', but the duke would have said 'Thornton's', it being the custom to name regiments after their commander.
5. Harrington, p. 47.
6. Ibid., p. 44.
7. Culloden House was the home of Duncan Forbes, a supporter of the King.
8. Harrington, p. 45.
9. *Life*, p. 104.
10. Harrington, p. 49.
11. Prebble, p. 31.
12. Ibid., p. 16.
13. Harrington, pp. 25-43.
14. Prebble, p. 25.
15. Harrington, pp. 33, 60.
16. Prebble, pp. 108-110.
17. *Life*, p. 104.
18. Prebble, p. 122.
19. Harrington, p. 83.
20. Prebble, pp. 137-140.
21. *Life*, p. 105.
22. Ibid., p. 104.
23. Prebble, pp. 236-7.
24. Hargrove (1789), p. 47.
25. Ibid., pp. 47-8.
26. Ibid., p. 48. (footnote)
27. W. Thornton, *The Counterpoise* (1752), pp. 23-5, 32-40.
28. Western, p. 106.
29. W.J. Kaye, *Records of Harrogate* (1922), p. xiii. (footnote)
30. *Life*, pp. 104-5.
31. Knaresborough Parish Register, C.R.O., Northallerton.

Chapter 10

1. G.A. Raikes, *Historical Records of the First Regiment of Militia* (1876), p.13.
2. *Life*, p. 106.
3. A. Kellett, *Yorkshire Dictionary of Dialect, Tradition and Folklore* (2002), p. 67.
4. *Life*, p. 106.
5. F. Wilson, *The Smuggling Story of Two Firths* (1993), pp. 14-15, 98-99.
6. *Life*, p. 107.
7. Ibid, pp. 110-111.
8. *The Life of John Metcalf* (1811), p. 57, footnote.
9. *Life*, pp. 111-112.
10. Ibid., p. 113.
11. W.J. Kaye, p. xxv.
12. W.E. Tate, F.B. Singleton, *A History of Yorkshire* (1960), p. 51.
13. Pawson, p. 173.
14. G.N. Wright, *Turnpike Roads* (1992), p. 9.

15. See, for example, Jennings, p. 286, following Smiles.
16. Order book (minutes) of the Harrogate-Boroughbridge Turnpike Trust (1752-1870), RT 43, Book 1, West Yorkshire Archives Service, Wakefield.
17. Will of Christopher Hopwood, butcher, of Knaresborough, 10 October 1729
18. Account book of the Harrogate-Boroughbridge Turnpike Trust (1752-1870) TD, 16, 1-12, MIC 669, N.Y.C.R.O., Northallerton.
19. *Life*, p. 115.
20. Ibid., p. 138.
21. W. Smith, *Old Yorkshire* (1881), Vol. 2. pp. 251-2.
22. H. Speight, *Nidderdale* (1894), p. 187.
23. *Life*, p. 115.
24. The replica, now in Knaresborough House, was made by Raymond Nudds and Albert Rolfe.

Chapter 11

1. 'Tut' is said to be a contraction of 'Tutelina', Roman goddess of corn.
2. *Life*, pp. 115-116.
3. *Life*, p. 116.
4. Measurements made by Geoffrey Craggs, whose garden in Fishergate includes the bridge.
5. J.L. McAdam, *Remarks on Systems of Making Roads* (1821). passim.
6. Reminiscence recorded by T. Sutcliffe, Smiles, pp. 230-231, footnote.
7. Account book, Harrogate to Boroughbridge Turnpike Trust, 13 December 1753.
8. Minutes, Wakefield-Halifax Turnpike Trust, 18 June, 11 August 1757.
9. Account book, 11 October 1752.
10. *Life*, p. 117
11. Information supplied by the late David Allott, who kept his donkeys in this field.
12. Copy of bill found in Knaresborough, in author's possession.
13. *Life*, p. 117.
14. Account book (note 7).
15. *Life*, pp. 117-118.
16. Ibid., p. 119.
17. J. Mayhall, *The Annals of Yorkshire* (1886), Vol. I, June 1753.
18. A. Raistrick, *Yorkshire Maps and Map Makers*, Dalesman (May 1948), p. 55.
19. Minute book, Wakefield-Halifax Turnpike, 11 September 1755, WYAS.
20. W. Albert, *The Turnpike Road System in England* (1972), p. 157.
21. 'The Rolling English Road', poem by G.K. Chesterton.
22. *Life*, p. 119.
23. Ibid., pp. 119-120.
24. Ibid., p. 120. Mr John Alcock is referred to in receipts and other accounts in 1764 held in Skipton Reference Library.
25. Minute book, Wakefield-Halifax Turnpike, September 1756, RT 105, WYAS.
26. *Transactions of the Halifax Antiquarian Society* (1937), p. 185.
27. A. Porritt, 'John Metcalf, Blind Road-Maker', *Transactions* (note 26) 1962, p. 25.
28. *Life*, p. 121.

Chapter 12

1. *Manchester Mercury*, 27 May 1755, advertisement.
2. *Life*, p. 123
3. Led by Colin Sidaway of the Adult Education Unit, 24 April 1993.

4. W.B. Crump, *Huddersfield Highways down the Ages*, (1949) pp. 80-81.
5. *Life*, p. 122.
6. Smiles, p. 228.
7. *Life*, pp. 123-4.
8. Smiles, p. 229.
9. W. Albert, *The Turnpike Road System* (1972), pp. 79, 137.
10. *Life*, p. 124.
11. Ibid., p. 125.
12. Ibid., pp. 125-6.
13. 'Day-Book of John Turner' (1760-62), MS 757, *Yorkshire Archaelogical Society*, E.G. Law, Eighteenth Century Huddersfield (1985), p. 4.
14. Ibid., p. 4.
15. Ibid., pp. 4-5.
16. *Life*, p. 135.
17. E. Bogg, *From Edenvale to the Plain of York*, (n.d.), p. 120.
18. Information supplied by Dr. George Redmonds of Lepton.
19. Bogg., p. 121.
20. Knaresborough Parish Register, N.Y.C.R.O.
21. Information supplied by Gay Oliver.
22 *Life*, p. 126. See also Trust Account CR 70/29/39-46, Local Study Archives, Chester.
23. Ibid., pp. 127-8.
24. *The Knaresborough Post*, 21 May,1999, quoting *The Macclesfield Commercial News*.
25. *Life*, p. 129.
26. Ibid., p. 128.
27. Crump, p. 81, *Life*, p. 130.
28. *Life*, p. 135.
29. H. Heginbotham, *Stockport Ancient and Modern* (1882),Vol L., p. 250.
30. *Life*, p. 135.

Chapter 13

1. *Life*, p. 131.
2. 'Nap'. A card game similar to whist, in which players declare the number of tricks they expect to take, up to five.
3. *Life*, p. 132
4. Ibid., p. 133.
5. Ibid., p. 134.
6. G. Bew, 'Observations on Blindness', *Transactions of the Literary and Philosophical Society of Manchester* (1782),Vol. 1, p. 172.
7. Ibid., p. 173.
8. Ibid., pp. 173-4, footnote.
9. Ibid., p. 175.
10. Ibid., p. 176.
11. *Life*, p. 130.
12. Order book, Wetherby-Knaresborough Turnpike Trust, 11 September 1783, RT 109, W.Y.A.S., p. 24.
13. Ibid., p. 20.
14. *Life*, p. 136.
15. Ibid., p. 136, Crump, p. 82.
16. W. Grainge, 'Yorkshire Eccentric Characters', *Old Yorkshire* (1883), ed. W. Smith,Vol. 1 V, p. 174.

17. See Crump, p. 82, P.S.M. Cross-Rudkin, *The Biographical Dictionary of Civil Engineers* (2002), p. 442.
18. Hargrove, op. cit. (1789), p. 65.
19. J. Wesley, *Journal*, 22 April 1788.
20. *Life*, pp. 137-8.
21. F. Campbell, 'Roads and Streets', *Bury Heritage Series No.2* (1982), p. 3.
22. 'The Blind Road-Maker of Bury', *East Lancaster Review* (1889), p. 95.
23. See photograph in pamphlet 'Toll Bars and Turnpike Roads of Bury' (1921), by S.W. Partington, p. 21.
24. *Life*, p.138.
25. *Life* (1812), p. 72.
26. J. Byng, *The Torrington Diaries*, Vol 3, pp. 44-5.
27. Smiles, p. 210, footnote.
28. *Life*, p. 138.
29. *York Courant*, 24 November 1771.
30. M. Worsley, 'Middlethorpe Hall', *Country Life*, 12 December 1985.
31. *Life*, p. 139.
32. *Universal British Directory* (1798), Vol. 4., p. 977.
33. Op. cit., (1812 ed.), p. 73.
34. *Life*, Preface (headed 'Advertisement' in 1795 ed.), p. vi.
35. Ibid., p. vii.
36. Ibid., pp. 139-40.
37. Hargrove, op. cit. (1798), p. 86.
38. *Life*, (1801), p. iv.
39. Hargrove, (1789) p. 229.
40. Information supplied by Margaret Powell.
41. Smiles, p. 231, footnote.
42. Teapot presented by Mrs J.S. Porter. Jack's 'stock' or white cravat, also presented to the council, has been lost.
43. I. Ousby, *James Plumptre's Britain* (1992), p. 95.
44. Ibid., pp. 94-5.
45. Hargrove, *Life of John Metcalf* (1811), p. 64.
46. All Saints Parish Register, Spofforth, MIC 1645, Vol. 9. N.Y.C.R.O.
47. G. Walker, *Costumes of Yorkshire* (1814), p. 87.
48. At the bottom of the inscription, below soil level, is inserted the name, 'Jno. A. Hilton', that of the monumental mason.

Chapter 14.

1. *Gentleman's Magazine* (1810), Vol. I, p. 597, *Eccentric Mirror* (1807), III, p. 24
2. Hargrove (1811), p. 3.
3. *Life of John Metcalf* (1812) ed. J. Kendrew, p. 72.
4. *Life of John Metcalf* (1812), ed. J. Johnson, Leeds.
5. A Hunter, *A Treatise on the Mineral Waters of Harrogate* (1830), pp. 16-17.
6. J. S. Wilson *Biography of the Blind* (4th edition) (1838), pp. 84-107.
7. Smiles, (1861), p. 225.
8. Ibid., p. 207.
9. Ibid., p. 229.
10. W. Grainge, *Three Wonderful Yorkshire Characters* (1864), p.17.
11. W. Grainge, *Yorkshire Longevity* (1864), pp. 77-83.
12. *Old Yorkshire* (1881), ed. W. Smith, pp. 170-174.
13. S. Baring-Gould, *Yorkshire Oddities* (1874), p. 85.

14. M. Searle, *Turnpikes and Tollbars* (1920), p. 90.
15. J.S. Fletcher, *A Picturesque History of Yorkshire* (1900), Vol. II, p. 234.
16. J.S. Fletcher, *The Enchanting North* (1908), p. 54.
17. J.S. Fletcher, *The Making of Modern Yorkshire* (1918), pp. 42-47.
18. J.S. Fletcher, *The Story of English Towns* (1920), p. 97.
19. Tate, Singleton, p. 53.
20. Albert, p.79.
21. Op. cit., article by P.S.M. Cross-Rudkin.
22. Op. cit., article by C.S. Hallas.
23. A. White, *The Years of Change* (1983), pp. 70-78, 84-87.
24. See p. 99.
25. Smiles, p. 231
26. *Life* (1812), p. 72.
27. Smiles, p. 210, footnote.
28. *Life*, p. 93.
29. Ibid., p. 37.
30. *Life* (1812), p. 19, p. 73.
31. Ibid., p. 19.
32. K. Jernigan, 'Blindness. Is History against us?' (1973) National Federation of the Blind homepage.

Mother Shipton dancing
to Blind Jack's fiddle.
(Caroline Miekima, 2000)

Appendix A: Blind Jack's Music

John Metcalf's fame as a road builder has eclipsed the fact that he was an acclaimed professional violinist and oboe player. Indeed, he played in public from at least the age of fifteen until the end of his life – a further seventy-seven years.

At least one of his viameters, two of his sticks and his teapot have been preserved, but where is Blind Jack's violin? Certainly it was known in 1914, when it was exhibited at an exhibition of 'The Art and Industry of the Blind', in Church House, Westminster, London, loaned by a Mr E.S. Metcalf. Enquiries through the helpful Metcalf Society and many other contacts have so far failed to track this violin down.

The actual music he played is almost as elusive. However, the general style of the eighteenth-century violin repertoire can be gathered, for example, from the manuscript tune-book inscribed Joshua Jackson's Book – 1798. Jackson, a corn-miller, lived just north of Harrogate at South Stainley and played his violin in the area known to John Metcalf, whom he is likely to have met and heard playing at the spa.

A selection of tunes and songs from this manuscript book was recorded in 1977 as *A Trip to Harrogate* by a group led by Bob Diehl, who with Gerry Murphy made the arrangements. More recently music from the same tune-book has been recorded by Magnetic North, a group led by Geoff Bowen, who once helped me to reconstruct Blind Jack's country dancing during a Knaresborough Arts Festival. ('The Miller's Jig', CD 005, is an excellent recording by Magnetic North, is available from Yorkshire Dales Workshops, 14 Oakburn Road, Ilkley, LS29 9NN, who have also produced a fine printed version of the Joshua Jackson MS.)

In the spring edition, 2007 of *EDS*, the magazine of the English Folk Dance and Song Society, Chris Partington suggests three of the tunes which Blind Jack 'could hardly not have known', namely 'A Trip to York', 'The Parson in his Boots' and 'The Game Chicken'. Amongst the 500 or so pieces we find in the Joshua Jackson tune-book are others which Metcalf would have known and played, such as 'Lovesick Polly', 'Tankard of Ale', 'Lovely Nancy', 'Morgan Rattler', 'The Morning Star', songs such as 'The Musical Lovers' and 'When War's Alarms', and 'Trips to Harrogate', 'To the Bath', 'To the Oatelands' and 'To Castle Howard'.

Two specific items mentioned by Blind Jack are 'The Frolicsome Sea Captain,' or 'Tit for Tat' (see p. 36) and 'Britons, Strike Home!' (see page p. 53) Both happen to be sea-songs, popular at this time because of their lively tunes.

Appendix B: John Metcalf's Roads

This chronological list of the roads made by Blind Jack is based on his own statements in 1795, on the surviving account and minute books of the turnpike trusts which employed him, and on a few confirmatory references.

In 1861 Samuel Smiles wrote that Metcalf had constructed 'nearly 200 miles' of roads, but then qualified this with a more conservative estimate of 'about 180 miles' – a figure accepted by P.S.M. Cross-Rudkin in *The Biographical Dictionary of Civil Engineers* (2002) This total presumably includes unspecified roads attributed to Blind Jack. The following list is largely supported by documentary evidence, but it cannot claim to be exhaustive.

Date	Place	Miles		Payment
1752–53	Minskip-Ferrensby	3		–
1753	(Tut Bridge, Boroughbridge)	–		–
1753–54	Knaresborough-Starbeck	1		£568
1754	Harrogate-Harewood Bridge	6		£1,200
1754–55	Chapeltown-Leeds	1		£400
1755	Skipton-Colne	4		–
1755	Colne-Burnley	2		–
1755	Broughton-East Morton	2		–
1755	Skipton-Addingham	2	(total)	£1,350
1756	Halifax-Wakefield	9+	(total)	£1,200
1756	Hag Bridge-Pontefract	3		–
1756	Crofton-Foulby	1		–
1756	(?) Pontefract-Doncaster (other work)	?	(total)	£6,400
1758–60	Huddersfield-Marsden, etc	20–30		£4,500
1760	Doctor Lane Head–Ashton-Mottram	16		£3,200
1760	(Housebuilding)			
1770	Macclesfield-Rainow-Chapel-in-le-Frith	8		£2,000
1770s	Congleton-Red Bull (with arches,walls etc)	6		£3,500
1770s	Poynton Park	5		£1,000
1770s	Whaley Bridge-Buxton	4		£2,500
1770s	High Flat, Pennistone	2		£340
1776–78	Huddersfield-Halifax	8		£2,700
1781–1783	Knaresborough-Wetherby	6		£980
1782	Congleton-Wilmslow	12		£3,000
1788	Marsden and Ottiwells Bridge	1		£1,000
1789–91	Bury-Accrington-Blackburn	18		£3,500

Note that Metcalf's work in many of these areas included not only the building of roads but also of drains, culverts, walls, arches, bridges and toll-houses.

Thieves Clough Bridge (built by Blind Jack in 1759).